Keiko Shokon

Keiko shokon, calligraphy by Nishioka Tsuneo

Keiko Shokon

Classical Warrior Traditions of Japan
Volume Three

**Edited by
Diane Skoss**

**Koryu Books
Berkeley Heights, New Jersey**

Published by Koryu Books
P.O. Box 86
Berkeley Heights, NJ 07922-0086
E-mail: ks3@koryubooks.com
http://koryu.com/
fax: 1-212-208-4366; toll-free tel: 1-888-665-6798

First printed 2002
Book and cover design by Koryu Books
Printed in the United States of America

Photo and illustration credits:
Cover photo of Yagyu Shingan-ryu demonstration at Meiji Shrine ©1999 Ron
  Beaubien.
Frontispiece calligraphy "Keiko shokon" by Nishioka Tsuneo; courtesy Phil Relnick.
Photos on pages 64, 73, 77, 79, 83, 88, 89, 90 ©2002 Ron Beaubien; photos on pages
  81, 118 ©2000 Ron Beaubien. Used with permission of the photographer.
Photos on pages 68, 71 from the collection of Nitta Suzuyo. Used with permission.
All other photos are from the collection of Meik and Diane Skoss; ©2002 Koryu
  Books.

Publisher's Cataloging-in-Publication
(Provided by Quality Books, Inc.)

Keiko shokon /edited by Diane Skoss. -- 1st ed.
          p. cm. -- (Classical warrior traditions of Japan ; 3)
          Includes bibliographical references and index.
          LCCN: 2001116543
          ISBN: 1-890536-06-7

          1. Swordplay--Japan--History. 2. Martial
    arts--Japan--History. I. Skoss, Diane. II. Series.

GV1150.K45 2002   796.86'0952
                                   QBI01-700483

To my family

Note on the Japanese in this text: Combine specialized terminology with a foreign language not written in the roman alphabet and you get quite a tangle. We have tried to establish and follow consistent guidelines; these are outlined in the "Koryu Books Japanese Style Sheet" (available at ftp.koryubooks.com as stylesheet.txt). Japanese names are given in Japanese order, surname first, except where the individual is a long-term resident of the West or is writing in English. Japanese terms (i.e. ones not found in *Webster's Third International Dictionary*) are presented in italics the first time they appear in each essay. Transliteration is based on a modified Hepburn system and long vowels are not specially marked. Japanese terms are translated where necessary in the text and translations are also provided in the index. Citations generally follow the *Chicago Manual of Style's* "author/date" system; parenthetical page numbers (with author and date where necessary) refer to items listed in the "Reference" section at the end of each chapter.

CONTENTS

Foreword viii
    Quintin Chambers

Preface ix
    Diane Skoss

Keiko Shokon Revisited: Introduction 12
    Diane Skoss

The Cat's Eerie Skill: A Translation of Issai Chozan's
    "Neko no Myojutsu" 17
    Karl F. Friday

Promise and Peril: The Potential of Following Multiple Koryu . . . 35
    Dave Lowry

Interview with Nitta Suzuyo: Headmaster of the Toda-ha Buko-ryu 63
    Liam Keeley

Challenges in Observing the Koryu Bugei 87
    Ron Beaubien

Itto-ryu Kenjutsu: An Overview 109
    Meik Skoss

Soke: Historical Incarnations of a Title and its Entitlements 129
    William M. Bodiford

Renovation and Innovation in Tradition 145
    Ellis Amdur

The Professional Perspective: Thoughts on the Koryu Bujutsu
    from a United States Marine 179
    George H. Bristol

Index 195

FOREWORD

People sometimes wonder why we devote so much of our lives to practicing these archaic combative arts. The articles and interviews in the first two volumes of this series, *Koryu Bujutsu* and *Sword & Spirit*, present the *koryu* in a way that is authentic and refreshingly devoid of frills and dramatization. This culminating volume, *Keiko Shokon*, confirms the thesis that the traditional combative systems of Japan can teach us and provide us with inspiration even in our modern technological society.

The koryu are characterized by a straightforward practicality. This is reflected in the way in which Diane Skoss has edited the material in these volumes; with the authority of one who has for many years studied and practiced the martial disciplines and who truly understands the essence of the koryu. Diane has inherited a mantle of hoplology, originally woven by Sir Richard Burton and brought out of obscurity by Donn F. Draeger. These three volumes occupy an important place in the literature and we can only hope that there will be more of the same from Koryu Books.

Quintin Chambers
Co-author of
Stick Fighting: Techniques of Self-Defense

PREFACE

This book, *Keiko Shokon*, continues where its elder brothers, *Koryu Bujutsu* and *Sword & Spirit*, left off. Together, the three volumes of the "Classical Warrior Traditions of Japan" series offer an overview of the state of the classical traditions. As with the traditions themselves, the viewpoints expressed in the essays in these books are varied, even contradictory — that's intentional. The only way to convey the myriad flavors of the *koryu* is through a diversity of voices. And in this latest volume, we've brought you more.

Readers of the previous volumes will find few differences; most notably, there's the absence of the "Ryu Guide." Space and finances dictated that we omit it this time, but we hope, in the future, to create a separate volume of short, illustrated articles on the most commonly encountered classical ryu. It's a long-term project!

We've also opted to use endnotes instead of footnotes. This was a difficult decision to make, since I personally hate having to flip to the end of a book chapter to read a note. Unfortunately, the length and frequency of notes caused sufficient clutter on the pages to force the switch. For those fans of footnotes, you have my most sincere apology.

This volume would not have been possible without the enthusiastic support of the readers of our previous books. Without you, *Keiko Shokon* would never have seen the light of day. Thank you!

The usual suspects once again offered consultation, commiseration, and coffee throughout the excessively long gestation of this book. In addition to my stalwart contributors, who never complained about my delays (though I fear I was rarely as circumspect), the lads and lasses at the Shutokukan and Itten Dojos lent their support at all phases of this endeavor. Thanks also to Quintin Chambers for his words of encouragement in the "Foreword." Suzanne Marshall, owner of Patewood Farm, and her horses, Banner, Tesoro Vistoso, Moose, Clark, and R.J. listened to far more than their share of my gripes. Lu Brezler, Steve Duncan, Lisa Granite, Steve Kelsey, John Mark, Yoko Sato, John Sims,

Derek Steel, and Bob Wolfe read the manuscript at various phases and offered their insights. Ubaldo Alcantara continued to pester me to get the book finished. To all of you, my heartfelt thanks!

Phil Relnick, my jo sensei, always says that we must have our priorities in the right order: Family, Work, Budo. I dedicate this volume to priority number one: Meik, Mom, Dad, Andy, JoAnne, Carl, Mark, and Mr. Wizard; and to all the members of my budo family — you know who you are!

Diane Skoss
March 2002

KEIKO SHOKON

*Diane Skoss began training in aikido in 1982 while at Indiana University finishing up Masters degrees in library science and English literature. In 1987 she moved to Tokyo; there she continued her aikido training and first encountered the classical warrior traditions. After a seven-year stint as managing editor of **Aikido Journal** and production manager for Aiki News' book division, she established her own publishing company, Koryu Books, and started the Internet website, Koryu.com. She holds the license of **okuden** in Toda-ha Buko-ryu and **okuiri-sho** in Shinto Muso-ryu, and has dan grades in jukendo, aikido, jodo, and tankendo. She returned to the United States at the end of 1997 and currently assists her husband instructing at the Shutokukan Dojo in New Jersey. She is also the assistant horse trainer at Patewood Farm, specializing in classical dressage.*

Keiko Shokon Revisited: Introduction

Diane Skoss

The first volume of "Classical Warrior Traditions of Japan," *Koryu Bujutsu*, aimed to answer the question, "Just what are the *koryu bujutsu?*" *Sword & Spirit*, volume two, explored the nature of these arts, their hearts and souls and the techniques that comprise them. In the third volume, *Keiko Shokon*, we turn our attention to the future of these arts. What role, if any, can sixteenth- and seventeenth-century Japanese martial arts play in the twenty-first century?

Margaret Stawowy wrote in her *Japan Times* review of *Sword & Spirit*:

> I can't help but wonder what relevance the classical martial arts have in the so-called civilized world, a world where warfare is waged impersonally with computer algorithms, or in the case of guerrilla combat, with increasingly sophisticated ballistics. (March 30, 1999)

This is a legitimate question answered in different ways by the essays in this volume. The koryu offer participants the opportunity to finely hone skills and assimilate standards that are no longer so commonly taught in modern society. Traditional values of perseverance, patience, constant awareness, self-effacement, working towards the good of a group rather than an individual, and appropriate, polite behavior contrast sharply with the get-it-instantly in-your-face brashness of the brave new world of the Internet culture. Nitta Suzuyo, nineteenth headmaster of the Toda-ha Buko-ryu, reveals in her interview with Liam Keeley her belief that training in the koryu promotes physical well-being as well as the development of precise and refined "people skills." Each execution of *kata* is a complex transaction in which both partners must instantly assess the opponent — discerning their current mental state, physical skill level, and intent — then adjust and react accordingly. With training this process becomes a deep and reliable intuition that can appear almost magical to the outside observer. What once was a skill on which a warrior's life might depend is now an invaluable tool for getting along with other people in all the various relationships and situations that we encounter daily.

The koryu have also provided the technical basis for modern sport forms of Japanese martial arts. Meik Skoss outlines the influence of the Itto-ryu on modern kendo in his overview of the tradition. Ron Beaubien demonstrates how properly developed observational skills can help inexperienced martial artists better appreciate those connections with the past and gain insight into their own training. If what you see isn't always what you get in the classical traditions, might this not also be true in modern arts as well?

Most Westerners involved in the transmission of the koryu (and undoubtedly most Japanese, too) are quite convinced that these arts are, at the very least, worth preserving as forms of self-discipline. The koryu, like the California condor, are too magnificent to allow to lapse into extinction. Yet as Dave Lowry points out in his essay:

> Like the conservationist who lovingly hand-rears a threatened species, thus rendering the offspring unable to feed and reproduce naturally as they should, he risks contributing to the weakening of the very institutions he loves so much and wishes so devoutly to preserve and propagate. (59)

Is the condor chick raised in captivity really the same fowl as its immediate ancestors? As twenty-first-century curators of sixteenth-century arts, we cannot afford to ignore such questions if the arts are to survive and thrive.

The critical issue is context and the native one for the koryu is that of feudal-era Japan. While many argue that modern Japan resembles old Japan no more than our Western culture does, that isn't strictly true. Many elements of the feudal era and the warrior culture do still permeate modern Japanese culture, and the Asian mind-set, with its Confucian and Buddhist influences, is vastly different from our Western way of seeing things. Modern Japanese culture is still the closest we can get to the native cultural habitat of the koryu, and it is a vital element in these arts' transmissions. The jury is still out on how successfully the koryu can be transmitted outside of Japan, as we are still in the first generation of that progression. Most of us who are directly involved are erring on the side of caution; to the extent that we possibly can, we are trying to instruct our students the way we were taught, forcing them to "step into Japan" when they enter the dojo. Americans, in particular, have a general aversion to relinquishing "inalienable rights," but in our role as conservators we must stalwartly resist any attempts to modify or adapt "the way things are" in the koryu to suit American notions of convenience. This "cast in stone" approach obscures the fact that the koryu have always adapted and evolved. Ellis Amdur investigates renovations and innovations and the question of whether it is ever appropriate to add something "new" to these "old" traditions, and if so, who might be legitimately qualified to make these changes.

Inappropriate change is not the only problem faced when the Japanese cultural background of the koryu is missing. Dramatic distortions and misrepresentations become easy in the West. Grandiose titles are part-and-parcel of the American martial arts industry; if one teacher advertises as a "Master" the next must perforce proclaim himself a "Grandmaster." On the next street over, the martial arts school operator suddenly becomes a "Great Grandmaster." Foreign terms have even more *caché* and selling power. Unwitting (at best — at worst, unscrupulous) Westerners have appropriated, misunderstood, and misused many Japanese terms properly applied only in very specific contexts. *Soke* (headmaster) has been perhaps the most blatantly (and laughably) misapplied. Dr. William Bodiford offers some definitions, explanations, and observations that can lead the non-Japanese martial artist towards a greater sensitivity to the nuances of Japanese language, history, and culture.

Like the museum curator or wildlife conservationist we must surround our charges with an environment as true to life as we can make it and educate visitors about the entire scene. But the koryu are not primarily cultural artifacts. They are ancient but effective systems for training for combat; their efficiency, however, is inextricably bound up with their methods of presentation and transmission — hence the need for cultural guardianship. Lt. Col. George Bristol discusses how the koryu curricula can actually apply in modern warfare — not the remote impersonality of Ms. Stawowy's query, but in the direct man-to-man combat of the Marine. Lt. Col. Bristol's observations illuminate yet one more side of the koryu's modern relevance, exhibiting innovation in its best sense by incorporating both pedagogy and philosophy into the newly developed Marine Corps Martial Art. His "ethical warrior" harks back to the "divine warrior" Issai Chozan describes in his eighteenth-century parable, "Neko no myojutsu," presented here by Dr. Karl Friday.

This kinship between warriors across the centuries brings us full circle. In the introduction to *Koryu Bujutsu* I first wrote of Nishioka Tsuneo's motto, *Keiko shokon*, most simply translated as "Reflecting deeply on the past, illuminate the present." Through study of the koryu, we find that the combative principles encoded in their kata are as valid today as they were four hundred years ago. The rigorous psychological and physical discipline required of the koryu practitioner continues to be an excellent forge for tempering mind, spirit, and body. And, although people and cultures have changed dramatically since the koryu's origins, the "ancient" social structure of the koryu still serves as a model of interpersonal relationships that can inform and enhance our modern social interactions. In short, the koryu, by offering a distillation of what was good and useful in the past, continue to provide remarkable lessons that we can use today to enlighten our understanding of who and what we are, and who and what we aim to become.

Karl F. Friday is a professor of history at the University of Georgia and is the author of **Hired Swords: The Rise of Private Warrior Power in Early Japan** *(1992) and* **Legacies of the Sword: The Kashima-Shinryu and Samurai Martial Culture** *(1997). He holds a* **menkyo kaiden** *(license of complete transmission) and is a fully certified* **shihan** *in Kashima-Shinryu.*

KEIKO SHOKON

The Cat's Eerie Skill
A Translation of Issai Chozan's
"Neko no Myojutsu"

Karl F. Friday

Turbulence and combat are a part of the lives of all creatures. From the smallest to the greatest, no species is utterly free of violence, least of all man, who has learned to kill not only for food or for self-defense, but in anger or hatred, for profit, and even for pleasure. Yet this creature, man, using the same hands with which he fashions tools of destruction, creates art that celebrates life; using the same mind with which he plots rapine, conceives philosophies that celebrate peace and harmony.

Among the myriad solutions mankind has proposed for taming its savagery none is as intricate or intriguing as the cultural and conceptual traditions surrounding the Japanese practice of the *bugei* (the military disciplines, or, more popularly, the martial arts). In late medieval and early modern Japan, martial training appropriated the status — as well as the forms, the vocabulary, the teaching methods, and even the ultimate goals — of religion and the fine arts. By the eighteenth century they had evolved into a complex cultural phenomenon in which various physical, technical, psychological, and philosophical factors were believed to intertwine and interact to produce a coherent path that guided both the physical and the moral activities of those who followed it.

The intricate entanglement of tactical, corporeal, mental, and spiritual concerns lies at the heart of classical Japanese martial art, and yet it is often only poorly understood. Scholars and aficionados alike have long been intrigued by the compelling paradox of samurai martial culture and its equation of perfection of the arts of violence with perfect non-violence. But to resolve this enigma, modern observers have tended to fall back on simplistic notions like an unattaching "Zen mind" that transcends and neutralizes the moral consequences of killing.[1]

While this idea is not entirely wrong, it misses a critical point: to the early modern samurai, proficiency in combat and spiritual enlightenment were not contending, or even sequential, achievements; they were interactive and interdependent developments — inseparable aspects of the same phenomenon — to be experienced simultaneously. It was, by this time, a fundamental premise of bugei instruction in Japan that the ability to utterly transcend any attraction to violence was *essential* to the perfection of combative skills. Pundits, drawing out the implications of a world view (formed at the nexus of Buddhism, Taoism, Neo-Confucianism, and Shinto thought) that stressed monism and the interpenetration of all things and all actions, were insisting that the study of fighting arts not only could but *must* eventually become a path to broader development of the self.[2]

One of the best illustrations of the reasoning that underlay this conclusion is Issai Chozan's eighteenth-century parable about the nature of ultimate proficiency in the fighting arts, *Neko no Myojutsu* ("The Cat's Eerie Skill"). Issai, whose real name was Tanba Jurozaemon Tadaaki, was a retired retainer of the Sekiyado domain in Shimosa Province (in what is now Chiba Prefecture), and a prominent scholar of Shinto, Buddhism, Confucianism, Taoism, and military science. He published *Neko no Myojutsu* in 1727, when he was sixty-nine years old, as part of a thirty-volume work entitled *Inaka Soji* ("The Country Chuang Tzu").[3]

The text centers on a discussion among a group of cats, concerning their failure to defeat an unusually ferocious rat. Issai uses the cats' skills and shortcomings as illustrations of successive levels of achievement in martial ability.

Keiko Shokon

NEKO NO MYOJUTSU

There was once a swordsman named Shoken, whose home was invaded by a huge rat that would appear and run about, even in broad daylight. Closing the rodent up in one room, he set his house cat to capturing it, but the rat charged, leaped at the cat's face, and bit her, causing the cat to squeal and run away. Nonplussed by this result, the swordsman borrowed several neighborhood cats who had made names for themselves as extraordinary rat-catchers, and turned them loose in the room. But the rat sat quietly in a corner until one of the cats approached, whereupon it leaped out and bit him. Seeing this terrible sight, the other cats froze with fear and could not advance.

The swordsman became enraged and, taking up a wooden sword, went after the rat himself to beat it to death. But the rat slipped beneath the wooden sword untouched, while the swordsman struck sliding doors and Chinese paper screens, tearing them to shreds. That spirited rat bound through the air with lightening-like speed, and even leapt at the swordsman's face, attempting to bite. At length, drenched with perspiration, Shoken summoned a servant. "I have heard tell," he said, "of a peerless cat about six or seven leagues from here. Borrow it and have it brought here."

The servant dispatched a man. But when he returned with the cat, the animal did not look especially clever, nor did its body appear in any way remarkable. Be that as it may, when the cat was placed in the room, the rat did not move from its corner, while the cat walked nonchalantly across the room, caught it, and dragged it back to Shoken.

That evening, all the cats assembled in the swordsman's home, with this Elder cat in the seat of honor. The other cats came forward, kneeled, and said, "We are all felines of some reputation, long-trained and skilled in this art. Not only rats, but even weasels and otters, we slap down and carve up with our claws. But we have never heard of anything like this ferocious rat. Through what skill were you able to bring it down? We humbly beseech you to share with us your wondrous art."

The Elder cat laughed and replied, "You are all young kittens. Although you are experts in your work, you have not until now heard tell of the methods of the true Way. And so when you meet with the unexpected, you are taken unaware. Nevertheless, let us first hear of the extent of each of your training and practice."

A shrewd black cat came forth from the group. "I was born," it began, "to a house of rat-catchers and have set my heart on that path. I can leap over a seven-foot folding screen or squeeze through a tiny hole. I have been unsurpassed in speed and acrobatics since I was a kitten. I can feign sleep or inattention, and have never failed to catch rats even when they run along the roofing beams. And yet today I faced a rat of unimaginable prowess, and was defeated for the first time in my life."

The Elder cat replied, "What you have mastered is rehearsed form. Thus you cannot escape your calculating mind. The ancients only taught technique in order to show the Way. And so their techniques and forms were simple and few, and yet they contained within them all the ultimate principals of the art. In this later age, many pursue technique and form exclusively, somehow or other putting together various tricks and mastering cleverness, while never equaling the prowess of the ancients. They use their talent, and contest one another in form and technique, but even the zenith of cleverness amounts to nothing. The small man, who perfects technique and concentrates on skill, must always be thus. Skill is the use of the body and the will, but it is not based in the Way. When one focuses on cleverness one falls into deceit, and often one's own skills and tricks are turned against oneself. Reflect upon this and learn it well."

Thereupon a large, tiger-striped cat stepped forward. "To my thinking," it said, "martial art requires the ability to move with *ki*.[4] I have, therefore, long practiced breathing exercises. I have built up my ki so that my *tanden* is firm and full — as if it reaches from Heaven to Earth.[5] I strike down my enemies with this alone, securing victory even before I advance to fight. I seize rats with it, answering their every attempt at change of tactic, just as the echo answers the voice it follows. I have no conscious thought of employing technique, and yet technique bubbles forth spontaneously. I can strike down rats running along ceiling beams just by staring at them; and then I take them. But this mighty rat came forth without form and left nothing in passing. What is one to make of this?"

The Elder cat rejoined, "You have trained at harnessing the impetus of your vital energy, but you count only on your ego. This is not the Good in the true sense of the Good. You go forth ready to shatter the enemy, and he comes forward to shatter you; what happens when he cannot be shattered? You seek to dominate and crush him and the enemy seeks to dominate you; what happens when he cannot be dominated? Why must it be that your will will always be strong and your enemies' always weak? The power that you think fills Heaven and Earth is but a representation of the real ki. It resembles Mencius' 'flood-like ki,' but it is not the same.[6] His is vigorous because it carries perspicacity; yours is vigorous because it is carried by your might. Thus its application is likewise different. It is like the main currents of the Yang-tze and Yellow Rivers or the might of a single night's flood. What happens when an enemy cannot be bowed by the force of your ki? It is said that a cornered rat will turn to bite a cat. He fights for his life, trapped, and with no other hope. He forgets his life, forgets his desires, and thinks only of the battle. He thinks nothing of his body. Thus his will is like iron. How can such an animal be made to submit by the force of one's ki?"

And then a gray, somewhat aged cat came quietly forward to speak. "As you say, though ki may be vigorous, it has portents. And that which has portents, however faint, can be detected. Thus I have long disciplined my heart such that I do not overawe or struggle; I harmonize and do not oppose. When the enemy is strong, I yield tranquilly to him. I engulf his technique like a curtain enveloping a stone thrown against it. I offer even the strongest rats nothing to fight. And yet this rat today neither bowed to force nor complied with yielding. It came and went like a ghost. I have never seen the like of this."

The Elder cat said, "What you are calling harmony is not a natural harmony; it is a contrived harmony. You seek to evade the enemy's attacking spirit, but when there is even the slightest presence of mind on your part, the enemy can perceive it. You self-consciously attempt to harmonize, and your spirit becomes muddied and lazy. When one acts out of forethought, one obstructs one's natural perception. And when one obstructs one's natural perception, sublime actions cannot come forth from anywhere. But when one follows one's intuition, without thinking and without doing, one has no presages. And when one has no presages, one can have no enemies under Heaven.

"But this is not to say that all of what you have trained at is of no value. If the Way permeates all its manifestations, all actions hold ultimate principle within them.[7] The ki activates the functions of the body. When the ki is magnanimous, it can harmonize with all things without limit. When the ki is in harmony, one ceases to fight with force, yet is not readily broken even when striking metal or rock.

"Nevertheless, where there is even a speck of self-conscious thought, all becomes artifice. This is not the naturalism of the Way. Therefore those you face do not capitulate, but become antagonistic. What sort of art should one use? Only be selfless and respond naturally.

"The Way has no ultimate. You should not think, from what I have said, that I have reached the zenith. A long time ago there was a cat in a village near mine. It slept all day long and showed no vigor of spirit. It was like a cat carved of wood. No one ever saw it catch a rat. And yet wherever that cat went, there were no rats nearby. It was the same wherever it had been. I went to it to ask why this was, but it didn't answer. Four times I asked and four times it gave no answer. It was not that the cat was ignoring me, but that it did not know *how* to answer. It did not know how it did what it did. What is known is not said, and what is said is not known. This cat had forgotten self and others. It had returned to a state of nonentity.[8] It was like King Wen of Chou, who attained divine warriorship, and killed not.[9] I am still far from attaining the level of that cat."

Shoken had been listening to these words as if dreaming. He then came forth and bowed to the Elder cat, saying, "I have long studied the art of the sword, but have not yet reached the ultimate in that path. But, having heard your ideas this evening, it seems that you have attained complete mastery of this path of mine. I beg of you: show me the inner secrets."

The cat replied, "Nay, I am a mere animal; rats are my food. What do I know of human activities? But one thing I once furtively overheard is that swordsmanship is not just about striving for victory over others. It is, in a phrase, the art that looks upon the profound and clarifies life and death. One who would be a samurai must always train in this art and nurture this will. Hence one must first permeate the principles of life and death, never deviating and never wavering, using no cleverness or thought, keeping one's heart and ki in harmony, without distinguishing self from others, and being undisturbed like the depths of a spring. Thus one will adapt and respond spontaneously to change.

"When the faintest thought of entities enters one's heart, there is relativity. When there is relativity there is an enemy and a self, who can confront one another and fight. In this state [one cannot] respond freely and spontaneously to change. One's heart has already fallen into the realm of death and lost its brightness of spirit; how can one stand and fight clearly in this state? Even if one wins, it would be but an accidental victory. This is not the true objective of swordsmanship.

"This state of nonentity should not be equated with an arrogant vacuity.[10] The spirit is originally without form; it stores no things. When it hoards anything at all, the ki will be drawn to that place. And when the ki is drawn to anyplace at all, adaptability cannot function unrestricted. It goes too much where it is directed, and it does not reach where it is not directed. Where there is too much, one's strength overflows and cannot be stopped. Where it does not reach, it starves and cannot be used. It cannot respond instantly with changes. The formlessness of which I speak holds nothing and is drawn to nothing. In it there is no enemy, and there is no self. It only responds to what comes, and leaves behind no tracks. The *I-ching* says, 'Without calculation and without artifice, being still and unmoving: this is what enables one's senses to penetrate all under Heaven.'[11] One who studies swordsmanship in light of this principle is close to the Way."

Shoken then asked, "What is meant by 'There is no enemy, and there is no self?'"

The cat answered, "There is an enemy because there is a self. Where there is no ego, there is no enemy. Enemy is simply a name for something in opposition, like yin to yang or fire to water. Wherever there is form there must be opposition. When there is no form in one's heart, there can be nothing to oppose it. When there is nothing to oppose one, there is no fight. Thus there is no self and there is no enemy. When one forgets both self and other, becoming like the undisturbed ocean depths, one is in harmony and at one with all. Although one strikes down the enemy's form, one is not conscious of it; nor is one unconscious of it. One is without deliberation and moves only with one's instincts. When one is completely unattached to all thoughts, the world is one's own world, and one makes no distinctions between correct and incorrect, or like and dislike. All these come from the line between pain and pleasure or gain and loss in one's own mind. Heaven and Earth are expansive, and yet there is nothing to be sought after outside one's own mind.

"The ancients said, 'When one's eyes focus only on dust, the Three Worlds seem shabby and narrow; when one's heart is carefree, one's whole life is rich and abundant.'[12] [This means that] when even a speck of ambition enters one's vision, one cannot keep one's eyes open. This happens when things enter into a place that was originally clear, and empty of things. This is an allegory for the mind and spirit. [Mencius] said that in the midst of millions of enemies, even though one's body can be crushed to dust, one's heart is one's own. Even a mighty foe cannot control one's mind and spirit.[13] Confucius said, 'Even a common man cannot be robbed of his will.'[14] If one is confused, this very mind aids one's enemies.

"This is all I have to say. Only reflect on it and seek yourselves. A teacher can only transmit the technique, and shed light on the principle. To realize the truth of it is in oneself. This is called 'acquisition through direct experience.'[15] It may also be called 'mind-to-mind transmission,' or 'transmission outside the teachings.'[16] This is not a matter of turning one's back on the teachings, for even the teacher cannot but convey them. Nor is it only Zen. From the lessons of the sages to the goals of the arts, all acquisition through direct experience is 'mind-to-mind transmission' and 'transmission outside the teachings.' The teachings themselves are only to point out what is already in oneself, albeit invisible. One does not receive such knowledge from a teacher. It is easy to teach, and easy to listen. But it is difficult to find what is in oneself and to make it one's own. This is called 'seeing reality.'[17] It is like rousing from an erroneous dream, and thus may also be called 'awakening.' There is no difference between these terms."

1727, sixth month, second day
Edo, Nihonbashi, Shinagawa-machi
Shojudo

In this compelling allegory, Issai describes the highest form of fighting ability as something beyond the achievement of physical skills, tactical brilliance, and even psycho-spiritual power. He identifies absolute, flawless proficiency in combat as a state in which one rises above all possible opponents by deactivating all possible opposition. The ultimate warrior is one in such perfect harmony with the natural order that he transcends both any interest in fighting and any need to fight.

This state is, however, qualitatively different from the sort of benign pacifism through strength commonly envisioned by modern, especially Western, martial art aficionados. The latter, exemplified by David Carradine's character in the popular 1970s television series *Kung Fu*, centers on the dismissal of aggression and ego, and on the deliberate avoidance of conflict. The consummate warrior of this ideal renounces war.

But in the classic Japanese ideal, a perfect warrior is still a warrior, performing the functions of a warrior, just as the master cat described in the parable was still a functioning cat. The cat kept its neighborhood free of rats, even though it did no overt hunting or killing. In the same way, bugei philosophers like Issai did not advocate abandoning the world and repudiating violence, the way a monk does, but *mastering* violence and becoming able to defend the realm and serve justice without needing to actually fight.

In *Neko no Myojutsu*, Issai not only characterizes what perfect martial skill involves, he illustrates why this must be the case. The cats of the parable describe increasingly sophisticated approaches to martial art, yet each approach is inherently and irredeemably flawed.

The swordsman's house cat appears to have relied on its physical strength and speed alone. But, Issai warns, no matter how strong or how fast one is, there will always be someone stronger or faster — as Shoken's pet quickly learned. This is precisely the reason that warriors develop martial arts and train in the first place: conditioning and the application of well-conceived tactics can enable relatively small or slow fighters to defeat larger or faster ones. The second cat in the parable had reached near-perfection of skill at this level. But, reminds Issai, while physical skills and tactical cunning give one a significant edge against most opponents, the very best will not be taken in; some will even find ways to exploit these devices to their own advantage.

A more sophisticated alternative to relying on either brawn or brain is to focus instead on developing sufficient psycho-spiritual presence to be able to dominate and overawe opponents into submission by sheer force of will. This is the line of attack favored by the third cat in Issai's tale. Becoming able to crush opponents with the power of one's spirit makes it possible to transcend corporeal limitations — for the spirit, unlike the body, need not weaken with age or illness. It also robs adversaries of any way to discern or anticipate one's stratagems — for there are none to be discerned. There is, therefore, an appealing mystique to fighting in this manner. Nevertheless Issai dismisses this as a relatively unreliable, and low-level, approach to combat. A more sophisticated method yet, is to focus not on overwhelming the opponent, but on yielding to him — deflecting all opposing force, and flowing around it like water in a stream. This gives opponents nothing to strike at, and leads them to defeat themselves. But even this, says Issai, falls short of perfect skill in martial art, for at this level non-violence is still an artifice that can be detected and exploited by an opponent.

Through the voice of the Elder cat, Issai argues that to reach the ultimate in combative skill — to place himself beyond all possibility of defeat — a warrior has to eliminate all self-conscious thought or guile, and act spontaneously, in complete harmony with Nature. Only by doing this can he free himself from reliance on physical, mental, or spiritual tools, and the risk of meeting an opponent who is better with them.

This premise is easy enough to understand, but the ramifications of accepting it are profound. For the desire to fight, to win, to see justice done, or even to survive are all manifestations of self-conscious thought, and all must be transcended in the quest for perfect martial art. And thus a journey that begins with a craving for certain victory must, if followed to its logical end, take one beyond outcomes, beyond fighting, and beyond even the self.

Notes

1   See, for example, Cleary, *The Japanese Art of War*; or King, *Zen and the Way of the Sword: Arming the Warrior Psyche*.

2   Excellent introductory discussions of premodern Japanese cosmology appear in Kitagawa, *On Understanding Japanese Religion*; Grapard, "Religious Practices"; Bito, "Thought and Religion, 1550–1700" and Najita, "History and Nature in Eighteenth Century Tokugawa Thought." For more on the relationship between cosmology and bugei thought, see Karl Friday with Seki Humitake, *Legacies of the Sword*, especially chapter 2.

3   Watanabe (7–8). Chuang Tzu was a Taoist philosopher and the author of a fourth-century BC collection of parables, anecdotes, and other moral lessons that bears his name. The complete text of *Neko no Myojutsu* is reproduced and annotated in Watanabe (10–16); the translation that follows is based on this version. A heavily paraphrased English translation of the text — missing several passages — appears in Suzuki (428–35).

4   Ki, or *ch'i* in Mandarin, denotes the universal and fundamental energy that, according to Sino-Japanese physiology, circulates within all living things. English-language discussions of the concept of ki and its application to Japanese martial art and other physical activities appear in Yuasa, *The Body, Self-Cultivation and Ki-Energy*, and Friday, *Legacies of the Sword* (153–55). Helen Hardacre, *Kuroizumikyo and the New Religions of Japan* (20–21), offers a brief, but illuminating discussion of ki as the term is used in modern Japanese culture and by Japanese religions.

5   The tanden (*tan-tien* in Mandarin; literally, "cinnabar field") is an important center for the collection and manipulation of ki, according to traditional Sino-Japanese physiology, said to be located approximately three centimeters below the navel. "Heaven and Earth" is a poetic metaphor for one's head and feet — that is, for one's entire body. The text uses the phrase "*tenchi ni mitsuru*" (literally, "filling Heaven and Earth") to describe the act of making one's ki reach from one's head to one's feet.

6   *Hao-jan chih ch'i*, or *kozen no ki*, in Japanese. *The Book of Mencius* describes this phenomenon as follows:

"May I ask what this 'flood-like ch'i' is?"

"It is difficult to explain. This is a ch'i which is, in the highest degree, vast and unyielding. Nourish it with integrity and place no obstacle in its path and it will fill the space between Heaven and Earth. It is a ch'i which unites rightness and the Way. Deprive it of these and it will collapse. It is born of accumulated rightness and cannot be appropriated by anyone through a sporadic show of rightness. Whenever one acts in a way that falls below the standard set in one's heart, it will collapse."

7   The phrase used here, "*doki ikkan*" (*tao-chi i-kuan* in Mandarin; literally, "the Way and the Vessels interpenetrated"), is an important Neo-Confucian construct that derives from a passage in an appendix to the *I-ching*, or *Book of Changes* (see note 11, below), known as the "Appended Statements" (*Hsi-tz'u ch'uan*, Japanese *Keijiden*) or "Great Commentary" (*Ta ch'uan*, Japanese *Daiden*) Part 1, Section 12: "What is above shape is called the Way, what exists under shape is called the vessels." An excellent translation of the entire passage appears in Rutt, 419–20.

8   *Mubutsu*, literally, "no-thingness." The phrase, "return to non-entity" (*mubutsu ni ki su*) comes from the *Lao-tzu* (also known as the *Tao te ching*), chapter 14.

9   Confucian tradition looks to the ancient Chou dynasty (?1122–770 BC) as a period of perfect governance, when the world was as it should be, and to King Wen (r. ?1099–1050 BC) as its most exemplary monarch. Wen was said to have the courage and martial fortitude of a god; his realm was always orderly and righteous, and yet he never needed to raise armies or kill enemies. The term rendered here as "divine warriorship" (following Suzuki, 432) is *shinbu*, a term of fundamental importance in Japanese bugei philosophy that might also be rendered as "divine valor," "true martial art," "spiritual martial power," or "sacred martialism." In its fullest sense, it describes the condition that holds when all the essential principles of martial art are put into application

simultaneously and in proper balance. It represents, in other words, the summation of idealized martial art. The term was being used in this context in Japan for many centuries before the advent of organized martial art schools. For more information, see Friday, *Legacies*, 63–65.

10 The cat is arguing here that non-entity (mubutsu) is a desirable, real-worldly thing that differs from the "arrogant vacuity" (*ganku*), the withdrawal from the world, preached by Buddhism.

11 The *I-ching*, or *Book of Changes*, is an ancient text of unknown origins. Cherished by both Confucians and Taoists, the text consists of explanations and commentaries on sixty-four hexagrams that symbolize the various states of Existence. Tradition holds that either the legendary King Wen (see note 9, above) or the Duke of Chou (r. 1042–1036 BC) wrote the main text, while Confucius added the commentaries, but modern scholars do not agree on when or by whom the book was produced. For details on the history of this text, see Rutt, 5–144.

12 The source of this quotation is unknown. "The Three Worlds" is a Buddhist term, referring to the three levels of existence: the world of desire, the world of form, and the world of pure spirit. In general, it indicates the entirety of the environment that living beings experience as part of life and death.

13 This sentence is a rather loose paraphrase of a sentence from the passage quoted in note 6, above.

14 This quotation comes from *Analects*, Book 9, Section 26. The full passage states, "The Master said, 'The Three Armies can be deprived of their leader, but a common man cannot be deprived of his will.'" The phrase, "Three Armies," appears in several places in the *Analects,* and seems to refer to an articulated force, with three wings, each under a separate commander, trained to carry out complex tactical maneuvers, such as encirclements and flank attacks. Mencius is drawing a parallel between the commander-in-chief of such a force — the "mind" of the army — and the will of an individual, arguing that the latter is inalienable. (Translation by

KEIKO SHOKON

Brooks and Brooks, *The Original Analects: Sayings of Confucius and His Successors*, 106.)

15 *Jitoku*, literally, "self-attainment," or "self-acquisition." Buddhists use this term to describe the learning of something through the experience of actually doing it.

16 'Mind-to-mind transmission' (*ishin denshin*) and 'transmission outside the teachings' (*kyoge betsuden*) are Zen Buddhist constructs referring to immediate insight into the nature of reality, based upon a student's immediate experience of that reality, guided there by his teacher.

17 'Seeing reality' (*kensho,* literally, "seeing nature") is a Zen Buddhist expression that describes the experience of awakening or enlightenment, similar in meaning to *satori.*

References

Bito, M. 1991. Thought and Religion, 1550–1700. In *The Cambridge History of Japan, Vol. 4: Early Modern Japan*, 373–424. Cambridge and New York: Cambridge University Press.

Brooks, E.B., and A.T. Brooks. 1998. *The Original Analects: Sayings of Confucius and His Successors*. New York: Columbia University Press.

Cleary, T. 1991. *The Japanese Art of War*. Boston: Shambala.

Friday, K.F., and H. Seki. 1997. *Legacies of the Sword: the Kashima-Shinryu and Samurai Martial Culture*. Honolulu: University of Hawai'i Press.

Grapard, A.G. 1999. Religious Practices. In *The Cambridge History of Japan, Vol. 2: Heian Japan*, 517–75. Cambridge and New York: Cambridge University Press.

Hardacre, H. 1986. *Kuroizumikyo and the New Religions of Japan*. Princeton, NJ: Princeton University Press.

King, W.L. 1993. *Zen and the Way of the Sword: Arming the Warrior Psyche*. New York: Oxford University Press.

Kitagawa, J. 1987. *On Understanding Japanese Religion*. Princeton, NJ: Princeton University Press.

Lau, D.C. 1970. *Mencius*. New York: Penguin Books.

Legge, J. 1969. *I Ching: Book of Changes*. New York: Bantam Books.

Najita, T. 1991. History and Nature in Eighteenth Century Tokugawa Thought. In *The Cambridge History of Japan, Vol. 4: Early Modern*

Japan, 596–659. Cambridge and New York: Cambridge University Press.

Suzuki, D.T. 1973. *Zen and Japanese Culture*. Princeton, NJ: Princeton University Press.

Watanabe, I., ed. 1979. *Budo no Meicho*. Tokyo: Tokyo Kopii Shuppanbu.

Wing-Tsit, C. 1963. *A Source Book in Chinese Philosophy*. Princeton, NJ: University of Princeton Press.

Yuasa, Y. 1993. *The Body, Self-Cultivation and Ki-Energy*. Albany, NY: State University of New York Press.

Dave Lowry is the author of **Autumn Lightning** *(1985),* **Sword & Brush** *(1995),* **Persimmon Wind** *(1998), and* **Moving Toward Stillness** *(2000). He has trained in martial arts for over thirty years; currently he is active in two koryu, the Yagyu Shinkage-ryu and Shindo Muso-ryu.*

Promise and Peril
The Potential of Following Multiple Koryu

Dave Lowry

Several decades ago, back in the forties — even before my time — the concert pianist Rosalyn Tureck made a singular announcement that fairly stirred the world of music. Having established a conspicuous reputation as an interpreter of several composers, Liszt, Debussy, and Chopin among them, Ms. Tureck nevertheless announced that forthwith, what remained of her professional career would be devoted exclusively to the performance of the works of J.S. Bach. It was an extraordinary move for a pianist of her stature. The decision occasioned, not incidentally, more than a little criticism from her contemporaries and others in the music world. But she was true to her word. At her concerts and recitals and onstage appearances, which continue to this day, she has played almost never again a note in public that was not Bach's.

I ruminate from time to time — most specifically those times when I am stumbling down the stairs of my home, bleary-eyed and searching for this weapon or that in preparation for morning practice — on Ms. Tureck's decision. Which day of the week it is will determine in which discipline my training partners and I will be participating. It is not as though, mind you, we have a smorgasbord of classical combative arts at our disposal. I am a member of and responsible for, to some degree, teaching only a couple of *koryu*. But when you consider the attendant and attached *ryu* that are a part of the training, that oft-times *uchi-* and *shidachi* are equipped with different weapons, and that even when they are not one must learn and practice and polish both sides... Well. Suffice to say the strains imposed upon an already easily overburdened faculty of memory and physical abilities that were never all that great to begin with conspire to make me wonder if Ms. Tureck isn't on the right track.

Many a reader will, I'd wager, find it difficult to evince much pity for the "lucky" exponent who has had exposure and experience in more than a single ryu. To launch upon a journey through the depths of a just one koryu would be, for them, the opportunity of a lifetime. To have trained in more than one seems almost an embarrassment of riches. That non-Japanese would have access to multiple koryu is even more astonishing in light of how very little time has elapsed since the days when even expert, experienced *budoka* in the West hadn't any idea at all that premodern Japanese martial arts existed, much less in how they differed, in content, structure, and aims, from the better-known budo — "better-known budo" being a relative term here. Less than forty years ago, judo and karatedo were still exotic enough for the masses. Indeed, the majority of the population in the United States or in Europe would have had difficulty distinguishing between the two. It wasn't just Westerners, by the way. More than once, in the late sixties and early seventies, well-meaning Japanese informed me that the samurai of old had honed their combative talents through the practice of kendo and that traditional ryu devoted to swordsmanship were now to be found only in TV and movie *chambara*. I graduated, from efforts at explaining that one of their countrymen was teaching me a classical system of the sword more than four centuries old (I'd have had similar luck trying to explain to an Englishman an apprenticeship in jousting), to a polite nod acknowledging, "Okay, if you say so." Now, less than two score years from that era and having just entered the twenty-first century, I am acquainted with close to a dozen Westerners who have had extensive exposure not to just the koryu, but to more than one. Extraordinary.

Those of us with this experience can alternately blame or applaud those who preceded our involvement and who actually made it possible. The first generation of *gaikokujin* to train in koryu in Japan — Draeger, Chambers, Relnick, and others — cleared a path. We of the second generation have followed along the trails they blazed. Followed them too, in that, just as they did, many of us have become involved in two or more koryu. The three above all trained in Shindo Muso-ryu and in Katori Shinto-ryu at least, and in other classical forms as well. Many in the second generation have also immersed themselves in a study of more than one koryu. It is on that subject that we convene here now.

A priori is to be established that, with very few and limited exceptions, this is a situation unique to our age and to the West. In Japan today, one can occasionally find a serious *bugeisha* who has trained in more than one koryu, though it is still unusual for reasons we shall detail presently. (The non-serious kinds of bugeisha, as common there as mimes at a street fair and only slightly less annoying, are another story entirely. "Masters" teaching a dozen different ryu have their goofy organizations and goofier acolytes in Japan; anyone believing the West is the only region so infested should get a load of these sideshows.) There are reasons, beyond the scope of our discussion, of culture, availability, and the general temperament of koryu teachers and authorities in Japan, to explain this scarcity. To undertake a study of another koryu after having entered and begun an apprenticeship in one would require no little effort on the part of the average Japanese practitioner. Introductions would have to be made (the easy part, since even in Japan the number of participants in these arts is not exactly overwhelming and there is, of course, a network of friends and acquaintances similar to what we have here). But because traditional martial ryu are far from widespread there, geographical proximity presents another significant obstacle. Even if there was the time available and the opportunity to train in another ryu, there may be none being taught anywhere near you. The chances of there being more than one, unless you were living in a metropolitan area like Tokyo, would be even less. The most critical impediment to adding a second ryu to one's combative repertoire, of course, would be that one's original teacher would be unhappy about the decision, which is to say he would, in all likelihood, have a full-blown hissy fit. His blessing being mandatory for you to go off and train in an additional tradition, that would be the end of the enterprise.

Whether, incidentally, this was the case during the feudal period in Japan, is another question. We know of numerous warriors during Japan's prolix medieval age, especially during the Tokugawa epoch (1603–1868), who expanded their martial education beyond the confines of one ryu. Drawing conclusions from this fact, however, absent the relevant cultural and historical contexts, viz. "They did it and to no harm and ostensibly to their benefit and so why shouldn't we?" are more debatable. First, martial ryu during the early part of the Sengoku jidai (1467–1568) must be evaluated in their *political* role as much as a means of transmitting combatively useful arts and techniques. Developed and headed by charismatic leaders, they attracted adherents who were influential and powerful and in turn, the ryu wielded substantial political power at the local fief or *han* level, at a provincial, and even on a national scale. (Tokugawa Ieyasu supposedly attributed the success of his regime to his adherence to the strategic principles of the Yagyu Shinkage-ryu.)

Second, early koryu also tended towards an inclusive approach to martial art. That is, the arts they taught and supervised were directed at entraining an initiate on a liberal spectrum ranging from the technical to the dispositional to the spiritual. These ryu sought to effect a desired transformation in the member, in the core of his being and personality. It is no exaggeration to say that an accomplished member of the Itto-ryu not only fought in a particular way, but perceived the world and organized his life around reifying principles of the Itto-ryu. He was absorbed into the ethos of the ryu. (This sounds vaguely Orwellian, I know. It is not quite that sinister or ubiquitous. No more so than in recognizing that today some aspects of our own personalities are shaped by the city or region in which we live, by our church or club affiliations, and by our work.) An expert of the Itto-ryu would respond to situations and would demonstrate traits that would have distinguished him from, say, an exponent of the Shinkage-ryu. The "personalities" of the ryu were different and it showed in their membership. This facet of koryu training would have obviously limited participation in more than one ryu — its ramifications are still a consideration, one to which we will return here presently.

In sum, an affiliation with a martial ryu during the Sengoku jidai had, then, political implications as well as providing an opportunity to further one's combative skills, and allegiance to one ryu was an expected, necessary convention of the period. Members identified with a single ryu. Leaving one to train in another was, at this time, primarily a luxury for some isolated individuals who wished to delve into the finer points of their arts or who were compelled to "round out" their abilities by learning the technical aspects of another system. A good example of this would be the swordsman who wanted to learn gunnery methods. He would hie himself off to a ryu specializing in the *tanegashima* to gain the mechanical expertise desired. (The paperwork needed for this kind of career enrichment program must have been daunting. Contrary to romantic images of the old samurai days, the Tokugawa regime was fanatically legalistic. Middle management drones as much as they were warriors for much of their history, for every enemy they cut down, it seems the samurai pushed at least a couple of reams of paper. A friend of my sensei's in Japan once showed me the petitions an ancestor had filed for permission to go off and revenge the murder of his father. The papers were more complex than a corporation's tax returns and were signed and sealed by nearly a dozen different bureaucrats.) Note, though, that it was the outstanding, experienced bugeisha who sought this extracurricular learning. He was already accomplished in one art before seeking another; he did not add the second to his repertoire *simultaneously*.

The average koryu practitioner had neither the time nor the inclination, however, for such ecumenism. There was a civil war going on, or, more accurately, a near-endless series of internecine conflicts unfolding. Combat was a constant concern. The overriding priority of the bugeisha was in obtaining the proper skills and a mental, muscular, neural, and spiritual foundation that would allow him to make it through the next campaign or coup or assassination attempt. That meant a near-obsessive concentration on a single system that was perfectible and dependable. It wasn't a climate amenable to dabbling or experimentation.

Later, during the latter half of the Tokugawa period, with its en-forced peace, the majority of koryu became attached to individual han. Political power was drained from the ryu and passed to these han and their *daimyo*. This evolution and the comparatively relaxed circum-stances of peace encouraged the bugeisha to sample other ryu where opportunities permitted. Surely, the inter-ryu matches and challenges that predominated martial activity during this era contributed to a less insular atmosphere among the bujutsu ryu. An exponent of the Kanemaki-ryu could barge into a Jigen-ryu dojo and request a match and, whether he got his butt handed to him on a *sanbo*[1] or whether he kicked those of the entire Jigen-ryu dojo, some learning took place. In those ryu that were under the direct control of the han, a koryu might also have had to accept, at the discretion of the daimyo, the presence of another school being taught where once it had a complete market share. The proximity of another ryu would have also led to some inter-ryu training and exchanges. Not surprisingly then, koryu dating from the eras following the Sengoku jidai sometimes reflect multiple influences.

Yet again, proper perspective is necessary to evaluate the resultant cross-pollination. Rather than creating an entirely new system, one ryu would be effectively subsumed by another. A good example of this can be found in the *fuzoku bugei* or "attached arts" of the Shindo Muso-ryu. Upper-level exponents of the school are taught, in addition to the jo and sword, the Ikkaku-ryu *jutte*, Uchida-ryu *tanjo*, and Isshin-ryu *kusarigama*. Each of these existed as separate ryu; each was gathered into the fold of the Shindo Muso-ryu during the Edo period (1600–1867) or later. Some members of the ryu insist these subsidiary arts are entirely separate and are taught as such. Clearly, however, the movements and principles of the *kata* for each demonstrate that in hav-ing been grafted onto the Shindo Muso-ryu tree, some, if not much, of their individual characteristics have been significantly altered, bringing them into harmony with the dominant nature of Shindo Muso-ryu.

Well, fields still further from our topic beckon. We amble back to ours having, I hope, established that while yes, martial exponents of earlier days in Japan may have experienced two or more ryu, the conditions under which they did so were substantially different from ours and that at any rate, they did not do so simultaneously.

No, the situation faced by Westerners learning simultaneously two or three or more koryu is unique. Never at any time or place in the history of the koryu as an institution have these two events occurred: a) there are non-Japanese practitioners intimately involved in them, even to the point of having been awarded teaching licenses in some isolated cases, and b) a goodly number of those foreigners have expanded their training to include a simultaneous study of more than one koryu. How it comes about that they end up practicing two or more ryu is worth a brief explanation.

It tends to happen like this: the number of Westerners involved with Japanese koryu is remarkably small. They all tend to know one another or, at the least, know *of* one another. And so, if you are among them and living outside Japan, comes a letter in your post box, a *ding!* at your e-mail, a call on the phone — probably during dinner. "Good news. Smith is relocating near you. Great fellow; we trained together in Gokiburi-ryu back in Nagoya. He'd like to meet you; can I put you in touch?" Of course and, as the proverb notes, those who have the same illness have much to talk about and not surprisingly you and Smith hit it right off. And while your interest to date in Gokiburi-ryu has been commensurate with, say, translating Urdu sonnets, presently you find yourself out in Smith's backyard, learning the rudiments of the Gokiburi-ryu. How can you not? One could, I suppose, say no thanks, I am studying Namako-ryu, find it eminently satisfactory, and wish to pursue it exclusively. There is more than a little something to be said for advocating this course of action, for limiting oneself to a single pursuit in these matters, as we shall discuss. But to be practical, it is like someone offering to give you an exquisite Chippendale bureau. Truth is you are interested only in American Windsor chairs. So what are you to do? Turn down the generous, perhaps once in a lifetime offer because English furniture of that period does not particularly turn your crank? Probably not. You find a place for the bureau. Begin to read about the style. You begin to appreciate the beauty and functionality of the Chippendale style, to understand how it reflected the spirit of the age in which it developed; to your mild surprise, you actually find yourself *liking* the stuff. (And mind you, as I said, we are talking only about the sorts of circumstances that occur here in the West. For non-Japanese koryu exponents living in Japan, these aleatory opportunities are far more plentiful.)

The fact is, like great antique furniture (though in many cases more perishable and delicate), the koryu are such a precious object, so rare, so remarkable, that many koryu practitioners feel, if nothing else, a sense of responsibility towards them. My analogy of the antique furniture is not entirely seamless, by the way. Some insist we do not inherit the ryu as we would an object, not whole and complete and without any needs for significant change beyond simply caring for it. They prefer to think it that we inherit the skills necessary to make that furniture. What we do with those skills, whether we employ them to copy painstakingly the furniture of earlier ages or whether we use them as an inspiration to create something new yet based thoroughly on older, well-founded principles, is a matter left to the predilections of the individual. I'll buy that. Doesn't matter; whichever way you tend to think of it, the conclusion remains unchanged. We have inherited *something*, clearly. And we are responsible for it.

The custodial inclinations of koryu members tend to extend to not only their own, once they join a ryu, but to koryu in general. When the occasion comes along to "collect" another one, the temptation for many is both real and understandable. I hasten to add that such an impulse toward acquisition is, it has been my experience, not at all like gathering a den full of bowling trophies or seeing how many stamps from the Republic of Gambia you can amass. There is little profit, less honor, in hoarding ryu to show them off like a butterfly collection and I can say honestly I've never run across a serious practitioner of koryu bujutsu who demonstrated that sort of attitude. The exponent who rattles off a list of koryu in which he has trained is more apt to be met with a politely concealed derision rather than respect from his colleagues. No, what we are talking about here is the experienced bugeisha who has been or is devoted to a serious study of two or three or more koryu. He has not sought them out, save possibly for his first. They

Keiko Shokon

have come to him, in a manner more or less as in the scenario I just described. He's got them. He's responsible for them to some degree. Now that he is, it is incumbent upon him to consider the ramifications, both good and bad, the perils and possibilities, of his choices.

That the Western koryu exponent in these opening years of the twenty-first century faces some problems and potentials that are unique in the long annals of classical Japanese combative disciplines is obvious. What is not so obvious is the multiple levels of complexity these situations present. Worse: the student is faced with the distressing circumstance of not knowing, even as he confronts them, which are the problems and which are the potentials. Imagine standing at the edge of a large field which may be, though you have no way of knowing: a) studded with diamonds yours for the plucking; b) planted with landmines; c) salted liberally with both mines and gems; or d) barren of either — and oh, by the way, you are to be blindfolded before entering. In a real sense, that is the situation faced by the exponent training in more than one ryu. He can never be sure that what he is doing is beneficial to himself and more importantly to the different ryu he's trying to master, or whether it is harmful, or whether it is, in the end, quite negligible.

What, exactly, are the problems and potentials? The koryu exponent who undertakes to study more than a single ryu must be very clear, as I said, about the dangers and rewards inherent in such a risk. Among them, a good place to begin is with the technical challenges presented by such a situation.

The dual exponent perceives, unconsciously or consciously, connections or correlations between the two ryu that may be valid and useful in his training or, just as possibly, invalid and destructive of his goals. Further, while the connections he sees or instinctively employs potentially *are* valid, they may be, as I said, inconsequential. If they are, focusing on them may well distract him from more salient and urgent aspects of his training.

There is a movement, in *ranken*, one of the sequences of the *tengusho* set of Yagyu Shinkage-ryu, in which the shidachi offers both hands to uchidachi, his sword held diagonally out in front. When uchidachi obliges by making a strike at the right hand, which is being held essentially as a bait, shidachi cheats the attack, dropping the right hand away to the side, clear of the angle of the incoming sword, then making a counter. The right hand dangles momentarily. The dodge isn't unique to the ryu; many others contain similar movements, often called *sasoi* or "inviting" postures or stratagems. Usually though, it's the left hand that drops away. When it does, most often that hand will be held open, pressed against one's side at about the level where the *saya* is slid into the belt. This movement with the empty left hand is a conditioned response. Even *kendoka* will do it automatically after having received instruction in the formal kata, when they perform the modern synthesized *seiteigata* or "standard forms."

When a student of the Shinkage-ryu is taught ranken, if he has prior experience in other ryu or in the kendo kata, he will, without conscious thought, press his right, empty hand close against his right side, rather than leaving it loose. He executes, in effect, the same response he has learned to do earlier, with his left hand. Now — and this is interesting from a variety of perspectives — what are the consequences of this inevitable habit? Again, the practitioner is faced with all sorts of possibilities. It's possible, certainly, that the right hand dangling loose in ranken is a weakness of the Shinkage-ryu, some defect that may have been transmitted through the generations and which, nevertheless, was left uncorrected all this time. It may be that originally the movement called for the same sort of hand against the side we see in other ryu. The right hand in that "standard" dangling, presumably correct position in ranken could be a recent development. Headmasters are human. Maybe one in the past had an arthritic arm and didn't like bending the elbow and so this unusual characteristic developed and was copied by his students and had been codified, even though it was not indigenous to the kata. (This is far from an extreme conjecture. Every ryu has stories of headmasters whose eccentricities have become enculturated, codified into the ryu.)

Maybe, on the other hand, there is something hidden here. The Shinkage-ryu exponent who places his palm on his waist automatically when the hand leaves the sword hilt rather than letting it dangle may be perverting an important part of the movement. He just doesn't know it yet because he has not been initiated into all the "real" meaning of the kata. Neither is this a wild speculation. Koryu teachers are notorious for allowing students to do a kata or a movement "wrong" for months, even years.

And on still the *other*, other hand (the conjugations here are numerous enough to tax the manipulations of Aizen Myo-o, the Buddhist deity with half-a-dozen arms), the gesture might be superfluous, might not matter a whit, one way or the other. That isn't the point, though, is it? The point is that the exponent doesn't really know. Doesn't know how much he ought to worry about this movement, how hard he ought to try to correct his way of doing it to conform to his teacher's, or whether it's not a big deal. That is the problem. A student training only in Shinkage-ryu could easily make a similar mistake, true. Still, it is much less difficult for a teacher to make corrections on the writing of a page he has supervised since it was blank than it is to laboriously erase mistakes or previous script that have been extensively entered on it before coming to him.

What, on the other hand, are the possible benefits, from a purely technical point of view, of training in more than one koryu? The most prominent advantage is that of a broadened and increased perspective on one's study. Studying two or three koryu, in this regard, is really no different from learning a second or third language. The learner perceives connections, draws parallels, makes faster progress because the lessons of one reinforce the other. No matter how widely disparate the ryu, all classical combative systems share at least some commonalties, giving the "two-fer" student twice the exposure to similar material. Pedagogical approaches, terminologies, even basics like gripping the weapon or simple movements overlap from ryu to ryu. His experience in one system informs that of another.

Cross-training in more than one ryu has a special potential when the two ryu have some close connection to one another. Representatives of the Kashima Shinto-ryu some years ago, spent time with senior exponents of the Katori Shinto-ryu, training in the latter's methods for quick-drawing the sword. These techniques had once been a part of the Kashima Shinto-ryu's curriculum, lost somewhere along the way. Since the ryu share a common root, efforts were made to "re-establish" at least some semblance of Kashima Shinto-ryu iaijutsu.[2] An exchange of this nature must have had some secondary effects on the members of the Kashima school, beyond merely re-creating their *iai*. Many other relationships in technique and strategy are shared between more than one school. These potentially could be strengthened and refined as teaching and training in one system informs the other. The finer points of *kiri kaeshi* could elude the student as explained and demonstrated by his teacher on Wednesday night training at the Ono-ha Itto-ryu dojo, but might appear perfectly explicable in the words or model of a teacher of the Hokushin Itto-ryu the same student sees on Saturday morning.

It's reasonable to assume that training in two schools that have no connection, historically or technically, could also be beneficial. The Hozoin-ryu is centered on the use of the spear. Ikkaku-ryu features a foot-long, hooked truncheon, used at very close quarters. A persuasive argument is to be made that learning one might balance the other, exposing the practitioner of both to wide varieties of distancing, timing, and so on. Similarly, a student of a school concerned primarily with weaponry could enlarge his understanding of combat by training in a koryu centered on grappling, like a jujutsu system. The curriculum of the Shindo Muso-ryu is a tradition of the stick and the sword, bereft of close-quarters combat. A study of the Takenouchi-ryu, which contains a broad repertoire of jujutsu, would be a natural avenue for the jodo exponent to explore. An historical precedence, arising from the exigencies of combat, for this kind of "one from column B, one from column A" approach does exist, as was noted above.

Bear in mind though, that this matter of having a wider perspective is a sword with two edges for the koryu member who doubles up. "Oh yes," he tells himself, watching a movement demonstrated for him for the first time in the Shimi-ha Mushibamu-ryu. "That's just like what's-it in Kabita-ryu." Uh-huh. Perhaps it is. Perhaps it only looks so superficially. Perhaps the principles behind the two movements from these two different schools are common. Perhaps they are not at all related. The student of two different traditions can fall into a serious trap by assuming correlations and connections that are not present or accurate. The making of such assumptions becomes a serious impediment to learning the new material and offers the potential of bastardizing what he has learned previously.

The practitioner of two or more ryu has not only the ancestors of one tradition looking over his shoulder; he has a couple, or a trio or more. When he begins to apply the *tai sabaki* of the Odori Kaba-ryu to his Fujitsubo-ryu, in his imagination he can happily envision the founder of the Fujitsubo-ryu beaming down and saying, "Yes, that's exactly what I was talking about. How fortunate this fine fellow has gotten the insights provided by Odori Kaba-ryu; it's provided a portal toward a mastery of my Fujitsubo-ryu." Just as likely, though, the Fujitsubo-ryu *ryuso* could be outraged from his position in the great beyond. "That tai sabaki isn't what this technique is all about, not even close!" He could conceivably be joined ethereally by the founder of the Odori Kaba-ryu who might commiserate, "Yep, he's not even doing the Odori Kaba tai sabaki correctly in the first place. Should have concentrated on it before messing up another ryu."

There is, then, a real risk of harm to both ryu when one applies the lessons of one to the other or attempts to extrapolate. The risk increases exponentially when the student "amalgamates" the different ryu he is pursuing. The cabriole legs of a Queen Anne table are unquestionably beautiful by any aesthetic standard. So too, the solid angles of a Hepplewhite bureau. It does not necessarily follow that grafting those legs onto the bureau will result in a superior piece of furniture. Just the opposite. The result is unattractive aesthetically, unreliable structurally, and utterly inauthentic historically. Cross-training, if it means a five-mile run in the morning, a kayak paddle in the afternoon, and a workout with weights at vesper-tide is a healthful equation. (For you, not for me.) Cross-training, if it entails practicing Tendo-ryu kata with a Shinto-ryu naginata while moving in the manner of the Tatsumi-ryu, is a disaster already unfolding.

Just as prominent as the risk for the double-dipper bugeisha of hybridization is the temptation to initiate "improvements" in one or another of the ryu he's pursuing. The student believes he sees a "flaw" in the Detarame-ryu he's just started, one that could be exploited by a technique or a principle from the Yamazaru-ryu he's being doing for five years. Yes, indeedy, he might be quite correct. He might also, however, be unable to see that Detarame-ryu has a method for overcoming this supposed flaw. His failure to recognize this could be because he hasn't yet reached that part of the curriculum dealing with it, or because his teacher has, for some reason or another, not revealed it, or because he's just too stupid to see it. So intent, in other words, on exploiting his broader knowledge, he may overlook the potential of the deeper lessons in the ryu.

The tendency to render a new and improved model has provided many an amusing highlight in the modern budo. I am thinking of the erstwhile accomplishments of a jujutsu "master" who, apparently after years of painstaking research and enormous expenditures of energy, has created a wonderful new theory of the art. His theory *is* interesting. Trouble is, the details of his marvelous "discoveries" are pedestrian knowledge to literally thousands of practitioners of jujutsu and even modern judo and aikido. This soi-disant master paddled at the shores of some combative arts, never swam in their deeper currents. The revelations he celebrates are merely poorly mapped charts of seas already known to those who had the perseverance to stick with a school or system long enough to sound the depths. Easily misguided by a superficial comprehension of a couple or more koryu, the exponent with such experience needs to be very careful in evaluating whatever insights he believes he's gaining and doubly cautious about implementing any reformations these divinations might inspire.

Mixing and matching koryu techniques, cross-training, and extrapolating one's own ambitious ameliorations: all are constant temptations when training in more than one koryu and all have conceivable benefits. Alternately, the consequences pose dangers that are not, for the most part, immediately apparent in most instances, making them all the more pernicious.

Obstacles, along with plausible benefits presented for the two-fer are not confined to the technical. They may influence the student's relationships with his sensei. *A result of training in more than one koryu may be that none of your teachers and others highly placed in the ryu may ever completely trust you.* It's understandable. The tendency is to wish to pass along family heirlooms to those in the family, not only in it but members of good-standing, who are unlikely to have divided loyalties or interests and whose undiluted resources are most likely to be expended in preserving the treasures and appreciating them to the fullest. Imagine yourself the headmaster of an ancient martial tradition, one who is not exactly, to put it politely, in the early innings of Life's pennant race. The limitations of time and energy are always a factor in taking on students for such leaders. Faced with a couple of prospective disciples, one of whom has no distractions in his practice, the other, a guy who has to duck out of the dojo's New Year celebrations to be off with his other dojo family — who's going to have the greater weight in your estimation?

Through the administrative efforts of organizations like the Nihon Kobudo Shinkokai and the Nihon Kobudo Kyokai, various koryu groups have, in the last half-century, enjoyed closer social relationships than ever in history. They get along and work together at regular demonstrations. There is, though, still a strong sense of individual identity in koryu. It isn't necessarily a sense of superiority (though I wouldn't be unduly hasty in ruling out that motivation). It is largely an abiding pride and a protective impulse for the ryu that keeps an attitude — "rivalry" would be a word too strong — fully cognizant of the ryu's uniqueness among all others as a focus of training and all aspects of participation. Ellis Amdur has explained why his own Araki-ryu teacher dropped out of the Nihon Kobudo Shinkokai. "Why," he asked, "would I want to be a member of an organization with a bunch of people who were from ryu that were, until recently, in competition against or were actually enemies of mine?" If a teacher doesn't even want to be a member of a general, overseeing body for koryu, and if the element of uniqueness is a primary facet in the overall structure of the ryu, how might the average headmaster feel about one of his students belonging to one or two others?

To be fair, several koryu headmasters and teachers have been very broadminded about allowing their foreign students to enter other ryu. Shimizu Takaji, the renowned postwar master of the Shindo Muso-ryu, initiated introductions for some of his non-Japanese students to train in other koryu. Other koryu authorities have been gracious and generous with their students, directing them to other teachers and actually encouraging a plural approach to the bujutsu. Still, the attitudes of exclusivity combined with an age-old reticence about sharing the technical details of one's ryu with another, present a formidable challenge for many koryu authorities in feeling entirely comfortable with their students moonlighting at another ryu.

The upside of not having your teacher completely trust you? Hard to imagine, but consider it this way: think back to the headmaster we just mentioned, deciding between accepting two potential students, one with no loyalties to other ryu, the other with membership in one or two or more ryu already. In making his decision, the headmaster might conclude he'd be passing along the corpus of his ryu best to the first student, who will be less apt to have other loyalties and priorities in his training. But he could decide the student with multiple memberships might have a wider and more exact idea of what koryu loyalties and priorities are all about. Given this wider experience, the headmaster could favor the second student and may form a closer relationship with him simply because the student walks into the dojo already well versed in the manners, sensibilities, and attitudes of a koryu exponent.

There is, to be sure, a plausible benefit of not being completely under the auspices of one teacher, of having one authority shaping, to a degree, one's personality and image of the world. Koryu sensei run the full gamut of Japanese society, in terms of their formal education, lifestyle, and in their basic nature as human beings. Some are urbane and cosmopolitan; others are provincial hicks. More than a few lead exemplary lives. Some are drunken louts. I have encountered koryu teachers I would literally trust with my life, others on whom I would literally not turn my back. Had I met and trained with only one, my image of the lot may have been skewed and one-dimensional, exactly as would have been my perceptions of koryu and its attendant Japanese culture. Likewise, my self-image was molded abundantly by the personality of my sensei. The contributions of other sensei and seniors in koryu and in arts like the tea ceremony and flower arranging were valuable in leavening, enriching, and contrasting the effects of his personality on me.

Additionally, the non-Japanese student of multiple ryu needs to consider the overall ramifications of his participation in the ryu and what it means to the ryu and to koryu in general. If Westerners are to have any sort of salutary effect on koryu, they must make their own contributions to it. Koryu are no different from other artistic impulses seen from an overall historical context. Their animating energies and motivations tend to ebb and flow. Periods of rapid growth and dynamic change are followed by years, even generations of quiescence and stagnation. One evening several years ago I spoke with one of the senior students of the Katori Shinto-ryu at the Narita dojo of the chief instructor, Otake Risuke. After talking about a number of subjects related to bujutsu, he asked me if I'd known the late Donn Draeger, who was the first foreigner to have trained in Katori Shinto-ryu. Sotto voce, he told me "Training hasn't been as hard since he was here." I had no doubt he was telling the truth. The Shinto-ryu had been in a long period of comparative quiet, located far out in the countryside and not a few of its members during the sixties and early seventies approached their training with the lukewarm enthusiasms of the dilettante. The personality of Draeger gave a jump-start to the ryu.

One of the reverberations of multiple loyalties among Western koryu adepts might be in galvanizing the previous generation, including the teachers, in reassessing their attitudes about exclusivity. This might be a catalyst for change sorely needed in koryu. Contrary to common criticisms of it, as an institution the koryu has never been fixed. Their fundamental structure and content may be more or less steadfast, yet when you consider the character for writing "ryu" is that of a "flowing stream" it is natural that, coursing through the centuries, alteration and evolution in these venerable traditions occur. As a group, non-Japanese exponents in the koryu have a tremendous potential for directing the flow of the classical martial arts through their interactions with their teachers. Otake Risuke once credited, among the influences of his Katori Shinto-ryu and in other bujutsu ryu, the tributary of Christianity that trickled into feudal Japan. That's a remarkable statement, acknowledging a non-Japanese influence on arts that many Japanese koryu authorities consider to be almost quintessentially "Japanese." Western koryu enthusiasts should consider it and reflect on the qualities of their own culture and civilization they may effect on their sensei and what this may mean for the future of the ryu.

For the exponent of two or more koryu, another consideration is the potential consequences his multiple participation plays from a personal, psychological standpoint. *The practitioner joining more than one ryu is susceptible to becoming disoriented in his goals and personal needs for training in a koryu.*

Take a spectator uninitiated into any aspects of Japanese combative arts to one of the *taikai*, the exhibitions of classical bujutsu held at various shrines or public gatherings like at the Budokan in Tokyo annually, and they'd be hard-pressed to distinguish one ryu from another.

The demonstrations all look alike to them: a series of people whacking away at one another. The ballistics of whacking being at least superficially limited, the morphology of whacking implements similarly so, this "it all looks alike" response is reasonable. Those who have some conversance in the koryu, who are, for example, not indifferent to the distinction between a *nagamaki* and a *naginata*, may be able to discern some more subtleties. Extensive experience, however, is necessary for the observer to make adequate conjecture about the different *intent* of the bujutsu demonstrated. Subtle and not readily apparent even to members of the ryu itself without a proper introduction, these different kinds and qualities of intent are absolutely essential in understanding the koryu and its aims.

The technical skills of fighting can be taught relatively easily. They are — this may surprise some readers — a limited facet of koryu training. The real challenge is in instilling the desired intent. By this, I mean not only an attitude that successfully copes with the demands of combat, but the ability to shuffle neurological responses in the proper order during the heat of combat in order to achieve the desired effect. So we're talking about koryu training not so much as a mechanical process, but as a specific designing of behavior. And those behaviors are specific and unique to an individual koryu. They are, in much more profound terms than its choice of weapons or particular techniques, the essence of the ryu itself. The behavior of the ryu exponent is what characterizes a ryu and distinguishes it from all others.

All sorts of factors influence the intent of a ryu. Social conditions, political necessities, the personal interests of the founder or the early headmasters can all play a role in the traits of a ryu, as can its overall principles and its preferred weapons. A jujutsu ryu specializing in weapons like a truncheon or short, weighted chain deployed against a swordsman may engender a "go for broke" personality in its exponents that demands immediate, overpowering aggression. A school of the naginata or spear could promote distinctly different combative traits in its members, with an intent of drawing or luring an opponent into range, "waiting" or forestalling an attack, or otherwise manipulating the situation to best advantage. One ryu may have been designed to produce combatants meant to perform as a unit; another could be directed at creating a martial artist who expected to engage in individual combat. Some ryu included sophisticated teachings related to troop deployment and some taught a "just go in there and kill the guy" approach. The strategy of a ryu, its overall intent, was meant to distill a certain personality. These are broad oversimplifications, obviously. No viable ryu would have been one-dimensional in its approach, just as no individual is always passive or consistently aggressive. Even so, the behavior or intent is what a ryu and all its training seek, and its teachings, in one way or another, are designed to produce that result.

To that end, generating a discrete behavioral pattern upon which the exponent can depend under the duress of combat means that an integration of techniques within a single system is crucial. Understanding on a neuro-muscular level this integration and the principles governing it is vital to developing a behavioral structure for the exponent. I hasten to add that this structure is as much psychological as it is physical; I separate the two merely to focus on specific aspects of the latter. When a martial artist engages in two different ryu, he must be aware of these intentions. Confusing one with another or attempting to mix them or trying to generate a hybrid intent is every bit as dangerous to the exponent and hazardous to the health of the ryu as are similar efforts to accomplish the same from a technical standpoint, which we've already discussed.

Finally, and most critically, when we are entertaining the problems and promises of seriously following more than a single koryu, we should look at the social and emotional ramifications to be found in such a multi-disciplinary pursuit. *The practitioner of two or more ryu is apt to develop a non-integrated personality as a result of his multiple training.*

After a dinner that lingered more than two hours over good food and better conversation one rainy night in Seattle (hard to imagine, I know; I'm assured the sun does shine there sometimes), Ellis Amdur, Meik and Diane Skoss, and I drove through dark, wet streets of the city, still talking. I steered them onto the topic of our present disquisition. All of them had trained extensively in Japan in more than a single koryu. All of them, in fact, teach more than one. So, I wanted to know, to which ryu did they feel the most intimate connection? Without the slightest hesitation each was able to tell me, when I asked them in turn, which ryu was essentially most "theirs"; the one that had most shaped their personalities and outlook on the world and molded the way in which they were most apt to run their lives and relate to others and to society in general.

Of a salient note here is a fact not well known among martial arts enthusiasts, even many of those who are widely read and knowledgeable about the koryu. I mentioned it earlier, describing the martial arts systems of the Sengoku jidai. Koryu, each of them, have distinctive "personalities." More to the point, they pervasively inform the long-time practitioner and member. (This is not a quality exclusive to the Japanese koryu. The more sophisticated the fighting art, we can fairly generalize, the more developed its personality. Nor is this always and necessarily a good quality. There are combative arts that are, to me, extremely impressive in their effectiveness. I would not for a moment, however, consider training in them. For me, the personalities they seem to embody and to germinate in their practitioners are psychologically disturbing, even dangerous. There are also arts that seem particularly suited, in the psychological perspective, to attracting individuals with disturbed personalities to begin with. The prospective student of any combative art should take this into consideration.) The personalities of the ryu go beyond the combative intent of its teachings mentioned previously. They are the collective psyche of the ryu. Martial koryu are not the only such traditional schools that have a distinguishable persona. With the right background and experience, an *ikebana* practitioner or a *chajin* can sit down with another exponent of those arts with similar or greater experience and in the course of half-an-hour's conversation, never having mentioned flowers or tea, can pretty reliably tell you from which ryu that person comes. That this is so is not a coincidence. It has entirely to do with the structure of a ryu.

In a real sense, joining a koryu (or any ryu) is like joining a family. I know modern budo organizations emphasize a similar goal and they may be structured deliberately to enhance familial-like relationships between members. Some of them may approach it and my sling is quite empty of aspersions. But I have been involved in budo organizations. And I have been a member of a koryu. There is a difference. In my opinion, the difference lies in the different motivations underlying the formation and maintenance of budo organizations and the ryu. The former invariably takes the model of a democratic (more or less) government, with officers, committees, and a large membership confederated through a few common interests. The ryu, conversely, is predicated upon the Confucian concepts of family. In Japanese, the word for an extended family is *ie*. Early ryu, many of them, were literally extensions of an ie, with members all stemming from one family. As they grew, the ie expanded and became *ichizoku roto*, a single family and its retained associates. The word for this group is *dozoku*. Dozoku organized for agricultural, military, or economic reasons, but what held them together was a shared ceremonial or ritual function. They held in common a veneration for the same ancestors to whom they may have been related either through blood or through a retainer kinship.

The ryu is a special kind of dozoku, gathered not expressly for the same reasons as other dozoku, although those certainly played a role in the history of most, but definitely sharing the dozoku's function as an extended kinship group with common ancestral bonds expressed through ceremonies or beliefs particular to them. In the koryu, the Japanese sense of belonging, of being a part of the group, is powerfully, dramatically exemplified, not only through these shared experiences, but also by the equally powerfully bonding process of mutual ceremony and ritual. It requires an effort to become a part of the group that is every bit as comprehensive as joining a family through marriage or adoption.

We mentioned previously how the intent of a ryu, the combative behavior it aimed at instilling, was a potent mechanism for creating at least part of a personality in the member. Beyond the intent of a koryu is its function as a dozoku, an extended family bound by both a common goal and a shared legacy of ritual. If koryu *are* families, let's apply the analogy to our koryu adept. He's married into the Smythe family, is participating as an accepted member of it. He knows his wife's sister will have a cow if the tinsel on the Christmas tree is flung in fistfuls rather than individually layered, knows her father needs to have his flask hidden the night before deer season starts lest he over-imbibe and fall out of the tree stand next morning, knows you can't seat Aunts Bessie and Edna together at the family reunion because Bessie voted for FDR and Edna never forgave her for it. It's all — you know very well what I'm talking about — being part of a family.

Now, however, our boy's decided he wants to join another. He wants to, if not marry a second wife, at least be a fully recognized member of the Mermelstein's clan who live down the street. You see the climb he has ahead of him? How many families can you belong to? Fit into? Fairly represent? Be effectively absorbed into their group mentality?

If a koryu were merely a collection of techniques, the participant would be limited only by the time available and the extent of other resources like his memory and physical stamina. If being a part of a family was nothing more than memorizing faces and names and attending the requisite weddings, christenings, and school graduations, and providing funds for bail when necessary, the same limitations would apply. But the commitments involved in really being a member of a family or a ryu imply far, far more. Becoming a member of both promises too, substantial reward, well beyond the mere accomplishments of just "belonging."

The critic notes that a lot of us *do* join second families and without visible damage beyond enduring terminally weird in-laws and tolerating the odd idiot brother-in-law. We marry. However, we marry and join a second family after having spent all our lives literally, developing a sense of ourselves, forming our personality, through the cohesive unit of our own clan. We don't grow up in two different families, precisely what the student of two different ryu attempts to do. Now, those same critics will again disagree, and point to the number of mixed families today, the products of divorces, second marriages, and Lord knows what collateral liaisons and living arrangements. Well, yes. And no more than a cursory observation of the travails experienced by the children of these convoluted unions is needed to see that it's a splendid argument against voluntarily getting involved in such a mess. Many of the same problems we've discussed about practitioners of multiple koryu — divided loyalties, confused identities, a fractured sense of one's own history — apply to children in these scrambled families.

By dividing his energies among two or more koryu, the adept with multiple memberships in them runs the real risk of eliminating a chance to penetrate deeply into the essence of the ryu itself. He's trying to marry into a second or third family without knowing much at all about his own. The profundities of insight, learning, and revelations about one's self and the world around him through participation in a koryu — I risk being patronizing here, so be it; I know what I'm talking about — are almost unimaginable to those who have not submitted themselves to an apprenticeship in a classical ryu system and then seen it through.

I was standing next to Nishioka Tsuneo at the end of a full week's worth of training, six hours a day. The septuagenarian has been at jodo for more than sixty years, a *menkyo kaiden* in and the seniormost practitioner of the ryu, and I let few chances to ask him questions pass by. "I don't understand how what the swordsman's doing in that kata would actually work," I said, nodding toward a pair performing it near us. "It wouldn't," Nishioka said instantly. "You have to change your footwork a bit." "Then why does the kata call for it done that way?" Just as quickly, Nishioka said, "I don't know. I'm still studying it."

This is the spirit of a koryu exploration. A lifetime refining, learning, contemplating, and *doing*. Within the realm of a single, seemingly narrow discipline, Nishioka has discovered the same depths Rosalyn Tureck has found in the works of Bach. Both are content to spend the rest of their lives investigating the nuances and wonderful complexities of one, relatively narrow field of endeavor. If an art has evolved to the point where people such as these are spending the better chunk of their tenure on the planet trying to plumb the depths of one, what do we face in attempting to pursue another ryu at the same time?

"Sad is the lot of the woman," reminds La Rochefocauld, "who is at once passionately inflamed and inflexibly virtuous." The koryu practitioner who trains in two or more traditions is similarly torn between what could be totally diverse inspirations. He runs smack into the awful notion, if he thinks about it, as he should, that his enthusiasms and ambitions to train in the different ryu made available to him could be chief among the threats most harmful to them and him. Like the conservationist who lovingly hand-rears a threatened species, thus rendering the offspring unable to feed and reproduce naturally as they should, he risks contributing to the weakening of the very institutions he loves so much and wishes so devoutly to preserve and propagate. In joining another ryu, he threatens its vitality. He makes enormous sacrifices to practice two or more, and ends up wondering if the most prominent contribution he will make to them is, in the end, bastardizing them more efficiently. It's a bite.

Entertaining and informative as our colloquy has been here, thanks in no small part to the erudition of the moderator, the whole thing does have the fusty, bookish odor of the theoretical about it, doesn't it? The fact of the matter is, most non-Japanese koryu members have at least a dual loyalty to another ryu family. Some of them rival Mormon fringe groups in their polygamous proclivities. Hectoring those who have the chance to add a second ryu to their schedule is likely to be as successful as a lecture on pudency delivered backstage to Las Vegas showgirls. Who're we trying to kid? If the opportunity arises, the koryu enthusiast is probably going to take it. When he does, though, he should be quite sober and fully apprised of the consequences, the pitfalls and possibilities that are inherent in his actions.

Conceivably, the koryu will meet more and greater tensions in the century just started than ever they have met in their long history. The contributions of non-Japanese will add dimensions to the koryu these arts have never before encountered. The individual Western bugeisha cannot, in a comprehensive way, do a whole lot to change substantially the flow of these ancient streams as they course into the new millenium. The currents of the koryu are sufficiently deep and set into their beds so as to frustrate any real alterations in their path by individuals. Whatever good or bad happens to them in a larger sense is beyond his control. He can, however, meditate thoughtfully and constantly about the repercussions of his practice and the results of his presence within koryu. And he can be particularly mindful that training in multiple ryu has a proportionally greater potential, for better or worse.

Just as dual training in koryu can have at least three possible outcomes, the Western exponent of bujutsu is likely to be regarded, at the beginning of the *next* century, in one of three perspectives. His twenty-first-century activities might be considered estimable. They might be disparaged and criticized and condemned to some degree for harm done koryu. Or the sum of his presence might be nil. As a means of preserving and propagating skills that can bring a human successfully through the most trying of situations, as worthy cultural repositories, as vehicles toward values timeless and universal, the koryu have proven themselves. It is now the turn of the Westerner who would learn the difficult lessons of these ryu, to demonstrate that he or she can prove themselves worthy of them.

KEIKO SHOKON

Notes

While I shall happily take credit for any accolades this piece might excite, its genesis and cultivation came as the result of many conversations and exchanges with Mesdames Diane Skoss and Kimiko Gunji and Mssrs. Muromoto, Amdur, Skoss, Lineberger, and Relnick, and any errors or flaws are to be blamed entirely on them.

1   A small wooden offering stand or tray.
2   See Chapter Nine, "Renovation and Innovation in Tradition" for a detailed discussion of this type of renovation.

*Liam Keeley is a member of the Toda-ha Buko-ryu, and has the license of **okuden mokuroku**, and the teaching rank of **shihan** in the ryu. He originally went to Japan to study budo in 1974 and lived in Japan for over twenty-two years. He is a member of the Board of Directors of the International Hoplology Society, and a regular contributor to the IHS's newsletter, **Hop-lite**. He is a founding member of the Japan Combatives Research and Discussion Group, a group of foreigners resident in Japan who meet informally several times a year to make presentations on the Japanese martial arts. Keeley now lives in Melbourne, Australia.*

KEIKO SHOKON

Interview with Nitta Suzuyo
Headmaster of the Toda-ha Buko-ryu

Liam Keeley

The following interview is an edited version of two interviews with Nitta Suzuyo Sensei on February 25 and March 20, 2001. The tapes are about four-and-a-half hours long, so in the interests of easier reading, irrelevant matter has been omitted, and where necessary, portions of the interview have been rearranged.

Nitta Suzuyo is the nineteenth *soke* of Toda-ha Buko-ryu. She was born in 1923 (Taisho 12) in Tokyo, where she grew up. She is a graduate of Toyo Kasei Jo Gakko. She succeeded Kobayashi Seiko Sensei as soke of Toda-ha Buko-ryu in 1981, and she is a member of the board of directors of the Nihon Kobudo Shinkokai.

Liam Keeley: Sensei, I was fascinated to read in Kendo Nippon that you remember, as an elementary school student, hearing shots one morning, and that you later discovered it was the abortive coup now known as the Niniroku Jiken.[1] You've certainly lived through a very interesting period of Japanese history.

Nitta Sensei: Yes. We lived near Tokyo Station close to the Imperial Palace. Early that morning we heard shots, but it didn't seem too dangerous, so it was decided that I should go to school anyway. On the way to school, we met some older students, who told us school had been cancelled, and that we should go straight home. We heard later that the [rebellious] troops had returned to their barracks. They had been told that the Emperor had commanded that if they returned immediately they would be treated leniently. Of course he didn't speak to them directly, but even so, in those days such a command carried unbelievable authority. People my age have many memories.

Nitta Suzuyo demonstrates the final "in your face"
zanshin movement, 2002

Would you mind sharing some of your memories of your teacher,
Kobayashi Seiko Sensei, with us?

I'd be very happy to do so. One is of her *kiai*, more particularly, the
yagoe (arrow voice) used by the senior in Buko-ryu to call the junior to
move in at the start of a *kata*. Her voice had an eerie, almost hypnotic
quality. Even when I was scared, or didn't really want to approach, I
felt compelled to start moving towards her. I also remember her fierce
intent. As you know, at the end of each of the *naginata* vs. *tachi* kata,
the senior student, who takes the role of the swordsman, moves in and
points the sword directly in the face of the junior. In the kata, the

sword "loses" to the naginata, but this move by the swordsman is a very aggressive, dominating one. I have such a strong memory of her explaining how the swordsman must express this domination in body language, as if calling out fiercely, *"Mada kuru ka? Mada yaru ka?"* (Still want to come in? Want some more?), as she did the movements.

Sensei, the other day you mentioned a saying by your teacher that impressed me, concerning the process of learning. Could you tell me more about it?

The phrase is *"Etoku, shutoku, taitoku"* (understanding, acquisition, mastery). It refers to the stages of learning; first you acquire the general idea or outline, then you practice, and then finally you internalize what you have been taught. But actually it wasn't Kobayashi Sensei who said that to me, it was my first naginata teacher, Ogiyama Shoji Sensei, a *shihan-dai* in Toda-ha Buko-ryu who was also a teacher at a regular public school. We lost contact because of the war, and we were so pleased when we finally met again many years later. After the war, he became a school principal.

Did he practice any other martial arts?

I believe he did some form of *taijutsu*, but I don't recall exactly what it was, and I suppose he had had compulsory kendo lessons at high school, as all the boys did. He was promoted [in Buko-ryu] relatively rapidly, and I think some of the women in the ryu were jealous of him, but I always felt he was a great help to Kobayashi Sensei.

How did you originally come to study naginata?

Shortly after I graduated from high school [1939], I went to a naginata seminar, sponsored by Kyobashi-ku, the local city ward — that's Chuo-ku nowadays. The seminar lasted five days or perhaps a week. If I remember correctly there were about twenty or thirty young women who attended. It was held at Kajichi Sho Gakko, a local elementary school. Ogiyama Sensei was the instructor, and I think there were three or four young women assisting him. Someone, I believe it was Ogiyama Sensei, asked me if I had done naginata before. I suppose it was because I had a certain familiarity with the weapon from my experience in *shimai* (an informal style of Noh drama). On the final day Kobayashi Sensei and Ogiyama Sensei gave a demonstration; I was absolutely enthralled. I really wanted to continue to study naginata, so I asked Ogiyama Sensei what I should do. He said that about half a dozen other girls had expressed an interest in continuing, and that he would be happy to teach us at the school. For a few months I went to the school to learn from him. One day it snowed heavily. At first I was the only student who came. I remember Ogiyama Sensei saying kindly to me, "Even if no one else turned up, I knew you would," which pleased me very much. However, after only a few months, he was conscripted. Before he left, he took the time to introduce me formally to Kobayashi Seiko Sensei, then soke of Toda-ha Buko-ryu, and asked her to accept me as a student. I was the only one of the group he was teaching who continued training under Kobayashi Sensei.

How old were you then?

I must have been about sixteen or seventeen. I had just finished school. I started rather late compared to many budoka. My teacher, Kobayashi Sensei, started when she was about five or six years old, but then her father, Chiba Chosaku, was a noted budoka with his own dojo. At first she didn't like training, and would cry and scream, *"Iya da, iya da, kirai!"* (No, no, I don't want to. I hate it!), when the time came for her lesson, but she gradually came to love the art.

What attracted you to the naginata in the first place?

It is difficult to say. I was a very quiet, rather introverted child. My adoptive parents encouraged me to study something. (I was born into the Katatae family, but I was adopted by my older sister, who was about sixteen years older than I. She had married a Nitta, and they had been unable to have children). I first took up the *shamisen* (three-stringed plucked lute), and later switched to the *koto* (plucked zither), before settling down to study shimai. For some reason, I was always very attracted to the naginata. I learnt the roles of Tomoe Gozen[2] and later Funa Benkei.[3] There was one more role in the school's

KEIKO SHOKON

repertoire, but the teacher didn't feel it was suitable for a young lady, so I never learned it. I was also discouraged from becoming a professional actress, since it wasn't considered a suitable career for me. When I first started to learn naginata, I was still taking lessons in shimai, so there was an overlap. I still have the naginata that my adoptive parents bought me to use for shimai. It cost thirty-odd yen, quite a lot of money in those days, and I can still remember how pleased and proud I was when they gave it to me.

Could you tell me about your training under Kobayashi Sensei?
After being introduced to her by Ogiyama Sensei, I trained for a short time at Kobayashi Sensei's dojo. However, soon after that, the dojo was destroyed, and we trained on an irregular basis at many different locations, often outdoors, such as on the grounds of various shrines. As women, we were lucky to have flexible schedules that allowed us to do this.

Was the dojo destroyed in the air raids?
No, it was torn down to create a firebreak. It may seem strange now, but because fires spread so rapidly through wooden buildings, the government ordered many buildings destroyed to create firebreaks. It was almost unthinkable to defy such an order in those days, and since no one was actually living in the dojo, there were no real grounds for protest.

The massive bombings of Tokyo must have been pretty scary.
Yes, they were. Our family home was destroyed by fire caused by the bombing in the last year of the war, on May 25.[4] We had previously helped some people who had become homeless in a big raid in March. We had let them stay with us, and lent or given them spare clothes and crockery and so on. Now it was our turn. As I said, our house was not far from the Imperial Palace. It may be hard to imagine now, but in those days the area around Tokyo Station was a regular suburb. I expect that the area around the Palace, or perhaps the Palace itself had been targeted. We fled after quickly soaking our clothes in the bath so

Kobayashi Seiko, previous soke of the Toda-ha Buko-ryu, ca. 1960

that they wouldn't catch fire from sparks. A lot of people fleeing the bombings had been badly burnt when their clothes caught fire, so we had this drilled into us. The bombardment was very intense. It was as if red snow was falling. My adoptive father was away. He had gone to Chiba Prefecture where he had relatives, to see if he could get us some food. Food was rationed in those days, and getting enough to eat had become difficult. He was terribly worried when he returned and found the house burnt to the ground. Luckily we met at a refugee center nearby the following morning. We had agreed on a place to meet in case of such an eventuality. Some of the people at the center were affected quite badly by the bombing. They were psychologically very distressed. At the time, I wasn't very afraid. I just thought, if you die, you die. To my embarrassment, some of the people at the center commented on the fact that I slept very soundly that night. I suppose many spent a sleepless night, but I slept like a baby. The next day, the trains weren't running, and we couldn't find any other kind of transport, so we walked from Tokyo Station to Nakano [a distance of about six miles as the crow flies; following the train tracks it is about nine miles]. There we were able to get a train to take us a bit further out to where we had some relatives whom we knew would take us in. The walk to Nakano seemed to take forever. My adoptive father had to stay downtown to be near his job at the Chiyoda Ward office. We were able to stay at my older brother's house in Mitaka for a while. He was quite shocked when he met us at Mitaka Station. I suppose we looked like the refugees we were. I was still wearing *zori* (straw sandals).

Do you have any other memories of the bombings?
  Yes, at one school where I taught, I arrived one morning to find that the school had been bombed and some people had been killed, including some teachers who had spent the night at the school. The bodies I saw had been burnt absolutely black, like charcoal. I was chased away by some soldiers who had been sent to clean up and take away the corpses. In those days they thought it bad for civilian morale for us to see such grisly sights. I suppose they thought that the civilian

population would become defeatist and clamor for an end to the war if they were exposed to such things.

How did you come to start teaching naginata?
During the war, the teaching of naginata to girls in the public schools expanded extremely rapidly. It was along the same lines as the teaching of kendo to boys. As a result, there was a shortage of qualified instructors and my teacher, Kobayashi Sensei, asked me to help out, even though I was comparatively new and inexperienced.

Could you tell us something of your schedule during the war years?
I was very busy. I was employed as a part-time teacher to teach naginata as part of the physical education curriculum for girls and young women.
I taught at a number of schools and colleges, among them Shika Daisen (a women's university of dentistry), Daini Shihan Joshi Gakko (a teachers training college for women), Nakano Kasei Jo Gakko, Kyobashi Kasei Jo Gakko, Shimogaya Joshi Shogyo Gakko, Asakusa-ku Musashimae Shogyo, and Asakusa Koto Jo Gakko. I found a copy of my schedule the other day and saw that I was teaching between twenty-four and twenty-six hours a week at various locations in Tokyo. It was quite a busy schedule, since that doesn't include traveling time. I was young, so I could handle it, but as food became increasingly scarce, it became more of a problem.

What was the attitude of the students?
At most schools I didn't have any problems, but I found teaching at the dentistry college rather intimidating, as many of the students were older than I. It was clear that they were just going through the motions and were not at all happy at being ordered to include naginata in their curriculum.

Budo is difficult enough to teach to willing students...
I'll never forget one day when I arrived and they asked me to give a lecture instead of the regular practice. I was completely unprepared to

Nitta Suzuyo demonstrating with Zama Shoko at Meiji Shrine, ca. 1982

lecture, so I just talked about how I had taken up naginata and what it meant to me.

That must have been tough; Japanese audiences can be very unresponsive. Maybe they needed the break. By that time, they were probably pretty good at sleeping with their eyes open...

Yes [giggles], I expect they just dozed through my talk. The women at the teachers college were easier to teach. I suppose they realized that they might be called upon to teach naginata in their turn when they graduated and became teachers.

What kind of techniques were you teaching? What was the curriculum? Did the individual teacher or ryuha get to decide?

No, it was a standardized (*seitei*) curriculum approved by the Ministry of Education. I imagine Kobayashi Sensei, as soke of Toda-ha Buko-ryu, and the headmasters and perhaps senior students of other schools of naginata, such as the Tendo-ryu and the Jikishinkage-ryu, were involved in formulating it. It is my understanding that they drew on Buko-ryu in particular for the basics as it was the only school that taught naginata against naginata in its basic practice. The *tsuki* (thrust) was supposed to be from Jikishinkage-ryu, and the *do-giri* (cut to the torso) from Tendo-ryu. I suppose they were very cautious and tried not to offend any of the major ryuha.

So you weren't actually teaching the koryu you yourself had been taught?
No, we did a lot of solo practice, repetition of basic techniques as in kendo, rather than the kind of paired kata practice that we do in koryu. It reflected the kind of kendo training prevailing at that time. Even at our own practice with Kobayashi Sensei, we only practiced the new standardized naginata. Some people weren't very happy, but we were forced to accept it.

How did you come to first start researching the history of Buko-ryu?
It happened in a rather roundabout way. One of my older brothers became interested in researching the history of our family. I was brought up in Tokyo, but my real father came from Kyushu. It seems that our family was quite prominent in the Isahaya area, not far from Nagasaki. My brother recently arranged for a family gathering commemorating four hundred and fifty years of family history that was very well attended. I thought that if he was researching our family history, I should try to do the same with Buko-ryu.

Could you tell us some of the results of your research?
It always seemed strange to me that the number of headmasters listed in our *mokuroku* (catalog of techniques awarded as a license) seemed far fewer than one would expect, given the length of time the ryu had been in existence, and I believe that I have cleared up that point. I was able to establish through research that there were nine names missing from the mokuroku I received, and I have decided that they should be included in future *makimono* (scrolls). We were aided by research done by Professor Yamamoto Kunio[5] of the University of Saitama. I have formally announced the results of my research in this

*Nitta Suzuyo with Toda-ha Buko-ryu
mokuroku*

regard to the board of directors of the Kobudo Shinkokai. As always, the late Muto Masao Sensei[6] was very encouraging and supportive of my research. I have also reviewed the names of the techniques listed in the naginata vs. naginata section of our mokuroku and changed the order. I believe that at some time in the past, the order changed owing to a misunderstanding, or perhaps a miscopying, and I have corrected that.

Another important result of research was the discovery of manuscripts and books listing techniques that had been lost. I have allowed my senior students, originally mainly Ellis Amdur with input from Kini Collins, Meik Skoss, and Zama Shoko, the freedom to experiment and try to recreate these techniques.[7]

Research has become a kind of ongoing hobby for me. Over the years I have become better organized. I wish now that I had kept better records right from the beginning. I sometimes find myself asking, "Wherever did I get this document from?" I can often recall the occasion, and from whom I received it, but sometimes I wish I had kept more detailed information regarding provenance.

Sensei, I know you are very much concerned with the succession, so for the record, would you please state the names of those to whom you have given teaching licenses?

Certainly. The first person to whom I gave a teaching license was Kini Collins, but we have lost contact, and I believe she is no longer active in budo. All the following have teaching licenses from me: Ellis Amdur (in the U.S.), Pierre and Claire Simon (in France), Meik Skoss (in the U.S.), Kent Sorensen (currently in Japan), and Liam Keeley (in Australia). Those who teach directly under my direction are known as shihan-dai, while those who are de facto independent as head of their own dojos I recognize as *shihan*, and to them I have given seals with which to authenticate any licenses they may choose to issue.

All foreigners...

Yes, that's the way it has worked out. As you know, at one stage I was bringing along a Japanese, a teacher licensed in another style, to succeed me as headmaster, and actually went so far at one stage as to designate him as my successor in Toda-ha Buko-ryu. However, he was never licensed in Buko-ryu, and there were a number of reasons why it didn't work out. I have formally notified the board of directors of the Kobudo Shinkokai that I no longer wish him to succeed me; instead I have designated my son, Shigeru, as my successor, although he has never practiced Buko-ryu. I have great hopes of another young Japanese man, but I feel he is too young at present for the responsibility of being headmaster; he needs several more years training. So, in a sense, my son Shigeru will act as a caretaker if necessary, until the headmastership can be filled by somebody appropriate.

KEIKO SHOKON

*Nitta Suzuyo demonstrating kagitsuki-tachi awase with Meik Skoss
at Kashima Jingu, June 1994*

How do you feel about having so many foreigners in Buko-ryu?

I've never thought of my students in terms of Japanese and non-Japanese, but rather as individuals. What is Japanese? I don't even know how Japanese I am. There are plenty of typically Japanese dishes that I don't particularly care for, but on the other hand, when I went to Denmark to visit my daughter Midori, I thoroughly enjoyed myself. I ate everything, and I certainly didn't have a problem with the food there. Let's say a foreigner comes to my dojo. Presumably they are there because they have an interest in koryu. There are plenty of Japanese who have no interest in the koryu at all. I feel I have been very fortunate, to have been surrounded by so many enthusiastic people who share a common interest with me.

Who are the people who got teaching licenses from Kobayashi Sensei?

Yamaguchi-san, Muto Mitsu-san, and myself were all given okuden. When Kobayashi Sensei became bedridden, I was appointed as shihan-dai, as her representative. There was some talk of me becoming soke then, but I didn't feel it was appropriate while she was still alive.

When did you become soke?

I was in my late fifties [1981]. As you know, there was some trouble about it, and Muto-san was not very happy about me becoming headmaster. She felt slighted that she hadn't been consulted, and after a period of time, she started teaching independently. She was Meik's first Buko-ryu teacher, and I have always respected the fact that he let a period of time elapse after her death before coming to me and asking to be enrolled as a student. I also very much respect the fact that although he had been ranked by Muto Sensei, he insisted on starting again from the beginning with me.

Could you tell us something of your education?

After I graduated from elementary school, I went to Toyo Kasei Jo Gakko. The principal of our school, Kishibe Fukuo Sensei, was quite a famous man, well known as an educator and author. He had once been granted an audience with the then-Crown Prince, who later became the Showa Emperor, which gave him tremendous status in those days. Although he himself had been overseas, and I believe he could speak English, we didn't learn any English, or indeed anything about foreign countries. Of course the thrust of education in those days was to turn us into good wives and mothers. The ability to keep house competently and do the household accounts and household chores was more important than anything else. We were told that it wasn't necessary for us to learn English, that other countries would have to learn Japanese. I wonder now what he really thought.

I think he was also very concerned about us having some accomplishments to show when we graduated. In those days, girls of good families were expected to have some kind of artistic skill or accomplishment, such as being able to play a musical instrument or be good

KEIKO SHOKON

calligraphers. Not to have any skill of this kind was a source of embarrassment. Perhaps that's why we had such a lot of calligraphy for summer homework. I remember once having to write out an extract from the *Rongo* (The Analects of Confucius) ten times. There were three hundred and sixty characters, and if you made just one mistake, you just had to start again from the beginning.

I do remember one exception to this disregard of things Western. In our final year of school we were given a formal Western-style meal as part of our education. I suppose it was so that we would not disgrace our husbands and our country by a display of ignorance of Western table manners should we have the occasion to sit down with Westerners at table. Although we were given a formal meal with all the courses, because of the war, all the portions were very small. It was rather strange, all those tiny portions on our plates.

You must all have been very shocked when Japan lost the war.
Yes, we didn't know what to expect, so we were all very nervous. We thought there would be a huge influx of American soldiers, and we didn't know how they would behave. Most parents were worried sick about their daughters' safety. I carried a dagger (*kaiken*) every day dur-

Nitta Suzuyo's kaiken

ing the last years of the war and through the first couple of years of the Occupation. It was given to me by my adoptive father, who was interested in swords. I was delighted to be given a weapon of my own and I still have it. At first I carried it more as a tool than anything else, thinking it would come in handy if I were trapped in a burning building or something like that, but during the Occupation I carried it as a weapon. I remember an inquisitive old man on the train who once asked me what I was carrying in my belt, and how he subsided into a shocked silence when I told him it was a dagger, with which I intended to defend myself.

In retrospect, I didn't think things out that clearly. I suppose I thought I could use it to defend myself if I were attacked, or use it to commit suicide as a last resort. As it turned out, I never needed it, and a class of girls who were quite happy to provide comfort to those American soldiers who wanted it soon emerged. When most people were poor, they were very well off from consorting with the victors, much better dressed and well fed, and they looked down on ordinary people, who in turn were scandalized by them.

Sensei, I know you are on the board of directors of the Nihon Kobudo Shinkokai. How long has Buko-ryu been associated with the Kobudo Shinkokai?

From the very beginning. Kobayashi Sensei was very proud of being a founding member. I seem to remember her saying it was founded in Showa 10. Last year we celebrated its sixty-fifth anniversary at the Nakano Sun Plaza, so it must have been started in 1935. There are quite a few members now, but in those days it was a rather small association.

There was a bit of a gap after the war, wasn't there?

Yes, the practice of budo was proscribed for a time, and after I got married, my husband was transferred to Nagoya, so I was away from Tokyo for about nine years. Travel was much more difficult in those days, and I was unable to train under Kobayashi Sensei for all those years. As soon as my husband was transferred back to Tokyo, I made contact with her and got back into training again.

Nitta Suzuyo at the Nakano Hombu Dojo, 2002

Where and when did you train after your return to Tokyo?

Again, we trained on a very irregular basis. She would telephone and make arrangements and then we would meet to train at all kinds of places at all kinds of hours. As the budo world gradually reorganized, I began to accompany her to all the demonstrations, and gradually became acquainted with other members of the Kobudo Shinkokai, such as Otsubo Motoharu Sensei[8] and Muto Sensei.

Many westerners are attracted to budo as a vehicle towards spiritual or at least character development. Do you have anything to say regarding this?

Well, I can only speak for myself. Looking back on my life, I'm very grateful to have had the opportunity to do budo. I think it has forced me to reflect more deeply about many things that I perhaps otherwise would have ignored or taken for granted. Obviously there are many benefits to training in budo, not the least of which is building a healthy body. My weight has remained almost exactly the same over the years. Of course, there are many ways to achieve maturity, and the way of modern budo, such as *atarashii naginata*, is one. But the koryu is another.

The very nature of koryu training, paired partner practice, means that one is faced with a wide variety of opponents/partners. They may be stronger or weaker, older or younger, technically more or less skilled, more or less experienced than you are. You have to learn how to assess and deal with all these people. It is up to you.

You know, when you get to my age, you start to reflect on many things. Budo is not just something to make you strong, or turn you into a good fighter. I feel very humble when I reflect on the many kindnesses and acts of friendship I have received over the years. Otsubo Sensei was always very kind and encouraging to me, even though I was not a member of his ryu. It was owing to him that we were able to get the space to train at the Nakano Ward Public Gymnasium. When I was new at the Kobudo Shinkokai, he was always encouraging. I re-member him saying to me, "When you do a *hono embu*,[9] it doesn't matter how technically skilled you are. Just do it with all your heart. Your school has good *reigi*, you can be proud of it."

More recently, Muto Sensei of the Yagyu Shingan-ryu has always been a very good friend and adviser. I'm very sad that he has passed away, he was so looking forward to the Kobudo Shinkokai demonstra-tion at the Asakusa Riverside Sports Center this spring.[10] He had some young women students whom he had asked to don colorful kimono specially for their demonstration. I think it was the first time that they were to demonstrate in kimono, and he had asked my advice about how they should tie their *tasuki* (cords used to tie back kimono

*Nitta Suzuyo with Muto Masao watching the demonstration
at Riverside Sports Center in Asakusa, April 15, 2000*

sleeves). Recently they and some senior students consulted with me about this again. They didn't want to go against his wish for them to demonstrate in kimono, but they felt they should wear something a bit more subdued than they had originally planned. In the end they decided to wear green-colored kimono. I'm so pleased to have been consulted and to be able to repay, even in such a small way, the many acts of kindness I received from Muto Sensei. He would often invite me to join him and other members of the Kinyobikai[11] for tea after a demonstration. He was such a thoughtful man; I remember, we once had a girl in our ryu who enjoyed a drink or two, and after a demonstration he would always unobtrusively delegate a couple of his students to keep an eye on her and make sure she got back home safely.

Do you think some people are more suited to one style than another? Many styles have very definite characters that I believe have a strong influence on those who practice them. Ellis and I have had some discussions about this in the past.

Yes, I do think that is so. However, something that has recently become more of an immediate concern to me is what I see as a misunderstanding of the purpose of kata training in koryu. It is important to understand that paired kata practice is not a *shiai*, not combat, nor is it a race.

Perhaps because nowadays there is no life or death combat using these weapons, there is a temptation to make training more competitive, more shiai-like.

Kata is not equivalent to shiai. You know, just before you came, I was watching TV, and I happened to see a variety program that featured an aikido teacher. I don't know who he was, but he had a very gentle face. He looked to be in his forties.

After he had done some impressive techniques, he was asked what he would do if he were attacked for real in the street, and he replied, "I'd probably run away." I thought that it takes someone really strong to say something like that. I was discussing this with my husband and I remembered that as a girl, with great daring, I had asked Kobayashi Sensei the same question. I expected her answer to be something like, "I'd knock the attacker down, of course," and I was very surprised when she laughed and said the same thing, "I'd probably run away."

Actually it sounds like a pretty professional response; assess the situation, stay cool, if necessary, run.

So, what are your concerns for Buko-ryu in the future?

I suppose my main concern is that the tradition I inherited be transmitted correctly and without change. I have always tried to teach exactly as I was taught, and when I explain techniques, I try to make clear to my students what is my personal opinion and what I learnt directly from my teacher. Even when I feel that I don't fully understand the rationale behind certain techniques, or think them strange, I feel strongly that it is my duty to pass on the techniques exactly as they were taught to me. As I said before, I have allowed some of my very senior students the freedom to do a certain amount of experimentation. I was so pleased recently when both Ellis and Meik said to me, quite independently, that after quite a long period of experimentation, that they had gone back to the old way of doing certain techniques. Of course, playing with technique, breaking down kata, can be very interesting. Most of the senior students are very good at that. My senior students often come up with very interesting interpretations and stimulating ideas. In the kata, there are all kinds of opportunities for skilled exponents to do

Nitta Suzuyo and her kaiken, 2002

ko-waza (small, intricate techniques). However, what can be done in the dojo under virtually ideal conditions, and what can be done on the battlefield, is very different.

Under less than ideal conditions, I believe that there is no time or place for small, intricate techniques. My own preference is for *o-waza*, big, powerful and committed moves to crush the opponent. This is what I would like to see my students do.

Nitta Sensei, thank you very much for sharing your thoughts with us.

Notes

1   The February 26th Incident was a coup attempt by a small faction of the military that occurred in 1936; several prominent political figures were killed, and martial law was declared in Tokyo to suppress the rebellion. The revolt lasted only three days, but it led to the rise of the military as an important political power in Japan.

2   Legendary naginata-wielding female warrior, first mentioned in the *Heike Monogatari*, whose story provided the basis for the early sixteenth-century Noh drama, *Tomoe.*

3   The famed retainer of Minamoto no Yoshitsune; Musashibo Benkei was said to be a huge and powerful warrior-monk, who was often portrayed wielding a naginata. A number of Noh dramas recount various apocryphal episodes in his life.

4   Much of Tokyo was destroyed in American firebombing raids during the spring of 1945.

5   Well-known scholar whose specialty is the koryu traditions of the Saitama area; author of several books on the topic.

6   Tenth headmaster of the Goto-ha Yagyu Shingan-ryu and successor to Otsubu Motoharu in his line of Yagyu Shinkage-ryu. Born in 1925, he died in March 2001.

7   To distinguish them from the *hon mokuroku* (main curriculum), which is what Nitta Sensei learned directly from Kobayashi sensei, these are known collectively as the *betsuden*, and cover the use of the *nagamaki*, *bo* (actually a broken naginata), and the *kusarigama* against the tachi (sword). The person with the sword is the teacher or senior. See more on the development of these techniques in Chapter Nine, "Renovation and Innovation in Tradition."

8   Otsubo Motoharu (Shiho) was a licensed independent instructor of Yagyu Shinkage-ryu; he died in 1993.

9   A demonstration, usually at a shrine, presented to the deities of the place. Reigi refers to methods of etiquette.

10   Demonstration held annually in mid-April; Muto died in March.

11   An informal meeting of researchers in the koryu, who convene every Friday (*kinyobi*) near the used bookstores in Kanda.

References

Amdur, E. 1995. The Development and History of the Naginata. *Journal of Asian Martial Arts* 4, no. 1: 32–49.

Ishigami, T. 1997. Toda-Ha Buko-Ryu Naginatajutsu Senka o Hasande Shugyo o Tsuzuke Tsuini Soke o Keisho Suru Hanashi (A Conversation about Toda-Ha Buko-Ryu Naginatajutsu). *Kendo Nippon* 253–254: 108–114; 116–122.

Skoss, M. 1988. Toda-Ha Buko-Ryu Naginata-Jutsu: Halberd Art From the Age of Warring States. *JMAS Newsletter* 6, no. 3: 2–7.

Ron Beaubien is an English teacher who serves as a part-time translator for martial arts demonstrations at the Nippon Budokan in Tokyo. A frequent contributor to the International Hoplology Society's newsletter **Hop-lite,** *he is also a member of the Japan Combatives Research and Discussion Group. Resident in Japan for over eleven years, he holds the* **okuden** *license in Toda-ha Buko-ryu naginatajutsu and trains in Tatsumi-ryu heiho.*

KEIKO SHOKON

CHALLENGES IN OBSERVING THE KORYU BUGEI

Ron Beaubien

Imagine two venerable codgers with wooden replicas of weapons from the days of yore. They move together slowly in an exaggerated ritual that bears little resemblance to combat. The audience is critical and dismissive: "Ridiculous. There's no way that would work in a real fight. What's so great about this stuff anyway?" This is how a surprising number of people react when they first see a demonstration of *koryu bugei* or classical Japanese martial arts.[1]

Indeed, my own first reaction was similar, though I believed I was reasonably open-minded and educated. I had read about the koryu bugei in the writings of Donn Draeger and had even watched a few of the classical Japanese martial traditions on video. I had trained for a number of years in karate. But at my first koryu demonstration, I saw one jujutsu tradition perform flailing, circular arm movements, with long drawn out shouts, and strikes that appeared to be performed with a loosely held fist and a bent wrist. These moves were in direct violation of the principles I had learned in karate.

One particularly outlandish movement occurred again and again in the various *kata* of this jujutsu school. The *tori*, or person performing the technique, forced his *uke*, the receiver, to bend backward. Then tori grabbed uke by the chest and waist, rotated him backward off his feet around in a full three-hundred-and-sixty-degree circle, and set the uke back down on his feet. It looked like a dance movement from the 1950s, and to my eyes, made no sense whatsoever. Although I knew relatively little about the system, I was confident that I had an idea about what was, or in this case, was not, effective for fighting. I was certain that what I had just seen would not be useful in a real fight, and I dismissed Yagyu Shingan-ryu as a worthless system....

Tori forces his uke to bend backward ...

... uke is forced off his feet ...

... momentum carries the uke upside down ...

... his body rotates to complete the circle ...

... uke is set back down on his feet.

Then, a few years later at the Nippon Budokan in Tokyo, I had the opportunity to see a demonstration by another line of the same tradition, under the leadership of the late Muto Masao, tenth generation *soke* of Goto-ha Yagyu Shingan-ryu. This time the technique was done a little differently. Instead of tori rotating his uke backward in a complete circle, the uke was instead turned upside down, his feet in the air with his body almost perpendicular to the floor. Then tori hesitated before turning uke back the way he came, finally dropping him onto his back on the wooden floor.[2] "Ah ha! A pile driver!" I thought. Suddenly this previously incomprehensible movement made sense. Perhaps the technique was practiced this way in order to keep from injuring or possibly killing the training partner who, in an actual combative encounter, would be summarily dropped on his head.

I was able to confirm this speculation through the illustrated works of Matsuda (103) and Higashiguchi (24). The technique, in fact, is a hallmark of the Yagyu Shingan-ryu and is often included as the final movement of many of this tradition's kata (Matsuda 117; Shimazu

90   KEIKO SHOKON

*Students of the late Muto Masao Sensei
performing the same technique*

48–88; Osano 134–181; Hoshi 46–81). I discovered that in the Tohoku lines of Yagyu Shingan-ryu, one of the names for the technique is *mukuri* [3] or *kaeshi* "turn over," while in other lines it is also referred to as *kaiten dosa*, or "rotation movement." I also learned that many of the techniques of Yagyu Shingan-ryu were designed to be performed while wearing armor, which explained a number of the unusual features of the performance. It simply had not occurred to me that many of the koryu traditions that specialize in armored combat often do not demonstrate in armor.

This experience illustrates just a few of the many challenges in observing the koryu bugei. Why is it so difficult to understand and evaluate these traditions? What factors must we consider while we are observing? How can one be a more educated viewer? Let's examine a

Challenges in Observing the Koryu Bugei   91

little more closely the various difficulties the average Western martial artist faces in his first encounter with a classical Japanese tradition.

OBSERVATION

The first pitfall, seldom discussed in martial arts circles, is simply that the observation and reporting of body movement is far more difficult than one might imagine. Not surprisingly, culture acts as a powerful filter that affects how we interpret what we see, and methodologies of observation have been developed by social scientists to try to counteract that natural tendency. Herein lie some clues. Since the 1950s, anthropologists, in particular, have explored and debated the advantages and disadvantages of observing culture from an insider's (emic) vs. an outsider's (etic) perspective (Pike 28-36; Wolcott 45). They have concluded that both of these vantage points can prove useful, depending on the conditions. For example, an outsider's perspective can be more objective, since it is slightly removed from the subject of study, while the insider's perspective is more appropriate when examining a private social group or subculture. Given the nature of the koryu bugei, the latter method of observation is preferred (Draeger 3; Friday 1997, 9). This is something more than merely "joining"; in order to observe effectively and evaluate the koryu bugei traditions it is necessary to make a long-term commitment to learn the tradition from within its original cultural context: a form of participant observation in the strictest sense.[4]

This commitment is required because culture acts as a paradigm. It shapes the way people view the entire world around them and defines the way they express themselves. Brenda Farnell, an anthropologist who traveled to Nigeria to research and document native dance, explained the difficulties she encountered while making observations in a local village:

> And then it happened: like Saul on the road to Damascus, it suddenly dawned on me that what I was writing down was what I thought they were doing — *I had no way at all of knowing what they thought they were doing.* In other words, I

KEIKO SHOKON

was busy interpreting and making judgments about the meanings of their body movements and their uses of the performance space entirely according to my own language and culture. Without being able to talk to the villagers in their own language, I could not possibly know what it all meant *from their perspective*... My naïve assumptions about 'universality' were completely shattered at that point and I stopped taking notes immediately, stunned by my newfound wisdom. I realized with considerable dismay that I did not possess the necessary skills to do what I was trying to do. (Farnell's italics, 146–147)

This is precisely the situation faced by a non-Japanese non-participant observer of the koryu bugei. Information is interpreted, then communicated to others through the lens of one's own culture, and this may well differ from how the people being observed see themselves.

Observation is also subjective. As illustrated in Kurosawa Akira's movie *Rashomon*, members of the same culture can view an identical scene but give conflicting reports immediately afterwards (Kebbell and Wagstaff; TLC). Part of the problem lies in an individual's perspective during the event and in their ability to recall what happened. Observational differences also arise based on where the observer focuses his attention, either consciously or unconsciously, within the overall scene. The feelings or thoughts an event arouses, and the observer's prior personal experiences also play an important part. In the koryu bugei, prior martial arts training often imposes a complicated bias, and this contributes to misunderstandings of Japan's classical martial arts.

KNOWLEDGE

Although today there are far fewer koryu bugei traditions than there were in the past, a wide variety has nonetheless survived. Each bugei *ryuha*, or school, is a product of the local culture, a result of geographical, social, and historical factors that have shaped it into its present form. Information was passed down selectively within each tradition and was guarded from outsiders.

Many of these martial traditions have long been isolated from one another, as the geography of Japan has never made travel easy. Its four main islands are heavily forested, two-thirds of the terrain is mountainous, and there is little arable land. Japan also receives plentiful rainfall and in the past large rivers were often rendered impassable after a heavy downpour. During the Edo period (1600–1868), for example, most travel was done on foot along major roads such as the Tokaido and Nakasendo, which ran from Edo — the present day capital, Tokyo — to Kyoto, the medieval capital. Even today many of the koryu bugei are still geographically isolated. A good friend of mine recently paid a visit to the dojo of Takenouchi Tojuro sensei in Okayama. Although he was taken by a Japanese driver who knew the route well, the drive was two hours out into the countryside from the closest city.

Many of the koryu bugei traditions were also separated linguistically due to this geographic separation. Even today, the Japanese language has many different regional dialects. Grammatical patterns, vocabulary, and intonation all vary from location to location, and speakers of one dialect often find speakers of another unintelligible (Shibatani 185). Although some koryu schools may at times share similar techniques and concepts, they often differ widely in the terminology used to name them, as in the Yagyu Shingan-ryu technique described earlier. Thus, a knowledge of the local dialect may be necessary to understand the techniques and the documents of a particular koryu bugei tradition.

Social restrictions also helped shape the koryu bugei that have survived. During the Edo period there were many bureaucratic and governmental restrictions on travel (Yamamoto 1). Barrier gates, known as *sekisho*, were placed along major roads to check travelers' paperwork. Regulations strictly controlled the movement of ordinary citizens, while samurai required a permit to leave their domain (Hurst 67). Although all classes of people had fewer restrictions when traveling on religious pilgrimages, the paperwork required to travel was always daunting. This further served to keep the koryu traditions isolated.

Many koryu bugei traditions have been practiced for generations in one specific locale and thus reflect the attitudes and beliefs of the people of the region. Koryu bugei schools often rose to prominence after being favored by a local lord or, in the case of Yagyu Shinkage-ryu and Ono-ha Itto-ryu, the shogun himself. Others, like Takenouchi-ryu, eschewed official appointments and were content to remain in the countryside (Takenouchi 52–54). Religious influences came from many sources including Shinto, Taoism, *mikkyo* (esoteric Buddhism), folk religion, and *shugendo*, the syncretic religion of the *yamabushi* or mountain ascetics. Tenshin Shoden Katori Shinto-ryu is a tradition well known for its connection to Katori Shrine, and also for the influences of Taoism and esoteric Buddhism.[5]

In addition to understanding a little about the cultural, historical, and social background of the koryu bugei, one needs to have a grasp of the technical aspects in order to observe them intelligently. The techniques of the koryu bugei have changed over time. Although each has its own philosophy and traditions, some of which members believe to have been passed down from the founder, techniques were added, removed, and lost over time. Some ryuha now retain only a small fragment of their original teachings, while others have curricula so large that no one person can master all of their kata in a lifetime of study. Without exception however, all of the koryu bugei ryuha have changed in some way over the course of time, even when change was not necessarily the intention. As intangible entities, the koryu bugei are of necessity shaped and changed by the personalities and experiences of the people that practiced and taught the traditions. This can be observed in the different lines of the same tradition, which often vary in the performance of common techniques, as in the case of Yagyu Shingan-ryu. In Takenouchi-ryu, a tradition that originated during the late Muromachi period (1333–1568), one may surmise that the original curriculum of the tradition did not include techniques for the *jutte*,[6] a short metal Edo-period truncheon used for restraining (Sasama 1982, 359–360), nor the use of *seiza*, which was not a sitting position in common use at that time (Osano 256–258).

The curricula of the koryu bugei are often very broad and the inner teachings are often not apparent from viewing the outer form (Friday 1997, 127). The koryu bugei are frequently quite esoteric. Secrecy was, and still is, a means of controlling information to prevent outsiders from learning the traditions' inner teachings. Often new members were required to give an oath of secrecy before entering (Dore 149–150; Otake 12). There were also schools, such as Owari Kan-ryu (Yokose 286) and Tatsumi-ryu (Kato 120), that were not allowed to be taught outside of their local domains.[7] In addition, most schools deliberately worded and illustrated their documents vaguely, so that they would be difficult for outsiders to understand (Friday 1997, 9, 137–145). The most important concepts or teachings were often not written, but orally transmitted by the highest-level initiates from one generation to the next. All of these methods were used in order to control the flow of information, and this further complicates the task of the modern observer.

PERFORMANCE

Fortunately, there are plenty of opportunities to observe the koryu bugei in Japan. Two of the most prominent organizations of koryu traditions are the Nihon Kobudo Shinkokai (Society for the Promotion of the Japanese Classical Martial Arts) and the Nihon Kobudo Kyokai (Japanese Classical Martial Arts Association). They are responsible for hosting a number of demonstrations each year. Founded in 1935, the Nihon Kobudo Shinkokai is a private organization run entirely by the participating traditions, while the Nihon Kobudo Kyokai, founded in 1979, is managed under the auspices of the Nippon Budokan in Tokyo. These two organizations alone present nine regularly scheduled demonstrations per year, and other demonstrations are organized by the individual schools themselves. However, one must be aware of the limitations of forming too definite an impression merely observing these koryu demonstrations; by their very nature they do not provide a complete representation of either the koryu bugei as a whole or the individual ryu.

Koryu bugei demonstrations are different from many modern martial arts exhibitions where individual techniques are combined to create an exciting display for the audience. Instead, koryu demonstrations are often considered offerings to Shinto deities, showing them that the classical martial traditions of Japan are being preserved. With this emphasis on preservation, traditional kata, or pattern practice — the primary method of training used for passing on knowledge from one generation to the next — are presented. The headmasters and various teachers of the koryu bugei are usually more concerned with making sure that their schools are passed on correctly than with pleasing an audience.

There are also some misconceptions about the techniques of the koryu bugei presented during demonstrations. Although kata may resemble combat at first glance, they are not intended to be actual combative scenarios. In Tatsumi-ryu, as well as in many other classical traditions, the lower level kata are used essentially for teaching new students the principles and fundamentals that will be needed later (Keeley 132–134; Skoss 1997, 133). Once these fundamentals have been mastered, more combative techniques are practiced in the middle and higher-level kata (Skoss 1997, 133; Skoss and Skoss 71). The lower level kata of many of the classical martial traditions are also the most often performed at koryu bugei demonstrations today. Thus, one is likely to see techniques that do not appear to be combative because they have been designed for training purposes rather than as tools for actual warfare.

The performance of kata by some traditions may also appear slower than others, but this should not necessarily be interpreted as a lack of skill. Teachers and headmasters of the koryu bugei differ in their opinions about the speed at which techniques ought to be performed. This is complicated by the fact that many of the koryu bugei currently demonstrate their armored techniques while wearing regular training gear because proper armor is rather expensive and difficult to obtain. Nitta Suzuyo, the nineteenth generation soke of Toda-ha Buko-ryu, has stated that she wants the techniques of her school to be demonstrated clearly. She feels that the techniques should be done without rushing quickly from one movement to the next. She emphasizes that each individual movement must be done with the proper speed, power, and timing. She believes that the techniques of the school were designed to be done while wearing armor and thus they simply cannot be performed at full speed. For example, *tosei gusoku*, the style of armor worn by *ashigaru* (foot soldiers) during the Muromachi period (1333–1568),

Challenges in Observing the Koryu Bugei   97

weighed from thirty-three to fifty-five pounds (Sasama 1992, 195). Vision is limited, the sheer weight of the iron helmet makes it difficult to move the head, additional stress is placed on the shoulders, and the torso is somewhat constricted. Deep stances are required for stability because of the need to balance in the top-heavy armor (Sasama 1992, 184 & 186; Spears 4–5). Likewise, it is possible to make many short, deft movements when using *bokuto* (wooden practice swords) or *fukuro shinai* (a bamboo training sword encased in leather) that are impossible when using a real sword. The sheer weight and momentum of the moving steel blade commits the user to the technique. Thus, the speed at which techniques are performed at koryu bugei demonstrations is determined by the desires of the teacher, the history of the school, and a consideration for the type of combat techniques being preserved within the tradition.

Although koryu demonstrations are very traditional, it is important to remember that they are still shows or exhibitions. The practitioners and techniques are pre-selected; more formal etiquette and attire are often used; the order, timing, and performance of techniques are evaluated or even altered beforehand; and care is taken to ensure that the demonstrations run smoothly. All of this preparation is done weeks or months prior to the presentation. Some teachers of the koryu bugei show techniques for which their school is famous or feature the wide variety of weapons contained in their schools' curricula, while others are content to demonstrate just a few representative techniques. As demonstration time is usually limited, with only ten to fifteen minutes, often less, per school at large events, many koryu traditions may only be able to present a small number of their techniques.

Just as the techniques may not be representative enough for an observer to accurately critique an entire system, the people chosen to demonstrate may not be capable of a fully representative demonstration of the ryu. Not every koryu bugei is able to send out its most experienced or most highly skilled practitioners for every demonstration. Many of the koryu bugei are quite small and some are currently being transmitted by no more than a handful of people in traditional farming communities. Those who choose to demonstrate out of obligation to their teacher and tradition often take time off work, and pay their own transportation and lodging costs. Demonstrating at a large venue, such as the Nippon Budokan, can cost each participant as much as one hundred US dollars in fees to the sponsoring organization. Costs for travel to and from the venue, shipping large weapons and armor, and hotel rates also add up quickly. These expenses, coupled with a small number of students, can prevent koryu bugei traditions from fielding their top practitioners or even from taking part at all in some demonstrations.

Demonstrations are also generally given by students who are in different stages of development. Some practitioners may be of advanced age and can no longer perform the techniques of the school with the full power and grace of their younger years. Ellis Amdur wrote about the Higo Koryu:

> It is sometimes hard for outsiders to evaluate or even partially understand another ryu-ha, particularly when the kata are performed by people of advanced years. They must either curtail their power to maintain their form, or lose their coordination while futilely trying to continue to cut with the power they had in their younger days. I have observed a film of Kino Sensei and her students and they have chosen (wisely, I believe) to maintain their form at the "expense" of the exertion of power. (52)

Children may also perform at koryu bugei demonstrations because such public performances are seen as part of the training process, where students learn to deal with the pressure of a stressful situation. Some koryu demonstrations are held with the younger practitioners in mind, and lower-ranking students are given their first chance to demonstrate at smaller venues, such as Yasukuni Shrine in Tokyo or the Okayama Kobudo Festival in Okayama City. The Nihon Kobudo Kyokai demonstration at Itsukushima Shrine near Hiroshima is also known as a venue where participation by less-experienced students is encouraged. Thus, any one demonstration may be the first for some, while others of the participants will have been demonstrating for much of their lives.

Koryu bugei demonstrations are wonderful opportunities to see many of Japan's classical martial traditions as schools gather from all over the country to participate. But one must never forget that what one is watching is a mixed bag. The participants are at various stages of their training and have varying skill levels. Not all schools are represented and the amount of technical material that can be presented is limited. And while the kata of the koryu bugei at times resemble combat, they are in fact primarily teaching principles believed to build the skills necessary for success in combat.

CONCLUSION

Modern technology has brought the koryu bugei to a much larger audience than the founders of these arts could ever have imagined. Video can capture and preserve moving images; airplanes can whisk us halfway round the world in less than one day. Although moving to Japan, formally entering a school, and training for many years is the best way to experience and understand the koryu, this is obviously not an option available to everyone. However, despite the difficulties of observation, the amount of knowledge required, and issues of performance, meticulous study of the correct sort can improve our understanding of this elusive subject.

Knowing the limitations of both content and participants in demonstrations can help head off hasty judgements. Carefully watching various live and taped demonstrations repeatedly over a long period of time is useful. Books can often be a good source of information, especially on the history of the koryu bugei. Although many ryu have been reluctant to reveal their techniques to the public in print, they have been willing to share the history of their arts. Documentary videos of the koryu traditions, though frequently expensive, are also helpful tools. Some of the Nippon Budokan videos, for example, focus on specific koryu demonstrations, while others are devoted entirely to an individual koryu school. Senior exponents of koryu schools also possess a wealth of knowledge. Listening to how long-term practitioners view their own arts can be of great advantage, and it may also provide the opportunity to get answers to specific questions not found elsewhere.

For those in Japan, the annual koryu demonstration at the Riverside Sports Center in Asakusa, Tokyo, includes several lectures by senior teachers of koryu traditions. These too can be helpful in enhancing a general appreciation of these arts.

Recognizing the difficulties involved in observing the koryu bugei is the first step in gaining a better understanding of the arts themselves. The koryu bugei have much to offer the modern world; it would be a shame to dismiss them lightly just because we lack the eyes to see them for what they truly are.

Notes

A great number of people have assisted me over the years. First, I would like to thank my family for always being there for me, despite my being away from home so long. James and Carole Morrone, Bill Phillips, and Carol Rahbari were also of great assistance.

For teaching me about the koryu bugei, I'd like to express my deepest gratitude to Nitta Suzuyo, Meik Skoss, Kent Sorensen, and Liam Keeley of Toda-ha Buko-ryu and in Tatsumi-ryu: Kato Takashi, Kato Hiroshi, Yamada Ichiro, and Liam Keeley. Likewise Watanabe Ichiro, the late Muto Masao, Irie Kohei, Okumura Shigenobu, and the other members of the Kinyobikai have also been most helpful in explaining the history of Japan's martial culture.

For assistance with this essay in particular, I am grateful to Diane Skoss for asking me to write for this volume and for her wonderful suggestions throughout the editing process. I am also indebted to Andrew Antis, Mike Ashworth, Antony Cundy, Susan Newton, Zach Smith, Derek Steel, and Mark V. Wiley for taking time out of their busy schedules to make thoughtful comments on various drafts of this essay.

1 Meik Skoss (1981) made similar observations when showing photographs and films of koryu bugei at shrine demonstrations to martial artists in the United States when he returned home for a short visit: "The general response was one of enthusiasm and interest in the beginning, leading to bewilderment, disinterest and wisecracks, and, finally, boredom."

2 A description of this movement performed in this fashion by the students of Muto Masao Sensei can also be found on pages 14 and 24 of the March 2000 issue of *Gekkan Hiden*.

3 The name mukuri, according to Matsuda Ryuchi, is a Sendai dialect word meaning *mekuri kaesu* or to "turn over" (Matsuda 103).

4 Further information on the methodology of participant observation can be found in the works of Spradley (1980) and Jorgensen (1989).

5 Practices of Katori Shinto-ryu that were influenced by religion can be found in Hall 274–292 and Otake.

KEIKO SHOKON

6   The English spelling "jutte" for the weapon is used here, rather than "jitte" which is preferred in many dictionaries such as *Kojien* or *Kenkyusha's New Japanese English Dictionary* because it more closely resembles the phonetic pronunciation favored by the Bitchu and main lines of Takenouchi-ryu (Takenouchi 181).

7   A further discussion of classical martial art traditions that were not allowed to be taught outside of their respective domains can be found in Osano, 177–182.

References

Amdur, E. 1994–1995. The Higo Ko Ryu: The "Old Tradition of Higo" and Kino Shizue Sensei. *Furyu* 1, no. 3.

Dore, R. 1984. *Education in Tokugawa Japan*. Michigan Classics in Japanese Studies, no. 8. Ann Arbor: Center for Japanese Studies, University of Michigan.

Draeger, D.F. 1979. An Introduction to Hoplology: Part II of II. *Hoplos* 1, no. 1: 3.

Farnell, B. 1999. It Goes Without Saying — But Not Always. In *Dance in the Field: Theory, Methods and Issues in Dance Ethnography*. Edited by T. Buckland. New York: St. Martins Press.

Friday, K.F. 1999. Kabala in Motion: Kata & Pattern Practice in the Tradition Bugei. In *Sword & Spirit*. Edited by D. Skoss. Berkeley Heights, NJ: Koryu Books.

Friday, K.F., and H. Seki. 1997. *Legacies of the Sword: the Kashima-Shinryu and Samurai Martial Culture*. Honolulu: University of Hawai'i Press.

Hall, D.A. 1990. *Marishiten: Buddhism and the Warrior Goddess*. Ann Arbor: University Microfilms.

Higashiguchi, T. 2000. Kansaiden (Hoshinden) Yagyu Shingan-Ryu. *Gekkan Hiden* 3: 24–25.

Hoshi, K. 1998. *Shoden Yagyu Shingan-ryu Hyohojutsu* (Correct Transmission: Yagyu Shingan-ryu Art of Strategy). Tokyo: Nihon Bujutsu Shiryokan.

Hurst, G.C. 1998. *Armed Martial Arts of Japan: Swordsmanship and Archery*. New Haven: Yale University Press.

Jorgensen, D.L. 1989. *Participant Observation: A Methodology for Human Studies*. Thousand Oaks, CA: Sage.

Kato, T. 1994. Tatsumi-ryu Heiho. In *Nihon Densho Bugei Ryuha: Dokuhon* (Japanese Martial Traditions: A Reader). Edited by Y. Miyazaki. Tokyo: Shin Jimbutsu Oraisha.

Kebbell, M., and G. Wagstaff. 1999. *Face Value? Evaluating the Accuracy of Eyewitness Information*. London: PRC.

Keeley, L. 1999. The Tojutsu of the Tatsumi-ryu. In *Sword & Spirit*. Edited by D. Skoss. Berkeley Heights, NJ: Koryu Books.

Kenkyusha's New Japanese-English Dictionary. 1974. Edited by K. Matsuda. Fourth Edition. Tokyo: Kenkyusha Limited.

Kojien. 2000. Fifth Edition. Tokyo: Iwanami Shoten.

The Law Commission (TLC). 1999. *Total Recall? The Reliability of Witness Testimony*. Wellington, New Zealand: TLC.

Matsuda, R. 1978. *Hiden Nihon Jujutsu* (Traditional Japanese Jujutsu). Tokyo: Shin Jimbutsu Oraisha.

Osano, J. 1994. *Zusetsu Nihon Bugei Bunka Gairon* (Illustrated Overview of Japanese Martial Art Culture). Tokyo: Fuyosha.

Otake, R. 1977. *Mukei Bunkazai Katori Shinto-ryu/The Deity and the Sword: Katori Shinto Ryu*. Tokyo: Minato Research.

Pike, K. 1999. Etic and Emic Standpoints for the Description of Behavior. In *The Insider/Outsider Problem*. Edited by R.T. McCutcheon. London: Cassell.

Rashomon. 1950. Directed by A. Kurosawa. RKO, Los Angeles.

Sasama, Y. 1982. *Nihon Budo Jiten* (The Dictionary of Japanese Martial Arts). Tokyo: Kashiwa Shobo Ltd.

———. 1992. *Buke Senjin Shiryo Jiten* (An Encyclopedia of Warrior Family Battlefield Materials). Tokyo: Dai Ichi Shobo.

Shibatani, M. 1990. *The Languages of Japan*. Cambridge: Cambridge University Press.

Shimazu, K. 1979. *Katchu Yawara Yagyu Shingan-ryu* (Armored Grappling Yagyu Shingan-ryu). Tokyo: Nitto Shoin.

Skoss, M. 1981. Problems of Perspective in Hoplology. *Hoplos* 3, no. 2: 2.

———. 1997. Tenjin Shinyo-ryu Jujutsu. In *Koryu Bujutsu*. Edited by D. Skoss. Berkeley Heights, NJ: Koryu Books.

Skoss, M., and D. Skoss. 1999. Field Guide to the Classical Japanese Martial Arts. In *Sword & Spirit*. Edited by D. Skoss. Berkeley Heights, NJ: Koryu Books.

Spears, M. 1999. Training in Armor. *Hop-lite* 8 (Fall): 4–5.

Spradley, J.P. 1980. *Participant Observation*. Fort Worth: Harcourt Brace.

Takenouchi, T. 1993. *Shinden no Bujutsu: Takenouchi-ryu* (Martial Art Transmitted from the Deities: Takenouchi-ryu). Tokyo: Gakushu Kenkyusha.

Wolcott, H.F. 1999. *Ethnography: A Way of Seeing.* Walnut Creek, CA: Altamira.

Yamamoto, H. 1993. *Technological Innovation and the Development of Transportation in Japan.* Tokyo: United Nations University Press.

Yokose, T. 2000. *Nihon no Kobudo* (Japan's Ancient Martial Arts). Tokyo: Nippon Budokan.

Meik Skoss is one of the foremost non-Japanese researchers and practitioners of the Japanese classical martial arts; his masters degree is in Physical Education. He began his martial arts training in 1966 in Los Angeles and moved to Japan in 1973. During his twenty-one year stay in Japan he received dan grades in a variety of Japanese martial arts, including jodo, jukendo, aikido, tankendo, and atarashii naginata. He holds the licenses of **okuden mokuroku** *and* **shihan** *in Toda-ha Buko-ryu and* **sho-mokuroku** *in Shinto Muso-ryu. He is also a member of the Yagyu Shinkage-ryu and Tendo-ryu. He teaches classical martial arts at his Shutokukan Dojo in New Jersey, and also serves on the local volunteer rescue squad.*

Itto-ryu Kenjutsu
An Overview

Meik Skoss

INTRODUCTION

Itto-ryu kenjutsu is one of the most significant schools of Japanese swordsmanship ever developed. It was chosen as one of the official *kenjutsu ryu* of the Tokugawa shogunate (Shinkage-ryu being the other). Many of the *daimyo* (lords of major feudal domains) throughout Japan also adopted it as an *otome ryu* (official system) for their own retainers.

In more recent times, the men instrumental in creating the technical curriculum of kendo (modern Japanese fencing, or swordsmanship with mock weapons made of bamboo) were greatly influenced by Itto-ryu theory and technique. Several of the men charged with creating the Dai Nippon Teikoku Kendo Kata, forerunner of today's Nihon Kendo Kata, were exponents of Hokushin Itto-ryu and they conferred with exponents of other branches of the Itto-ryu in order to create the forms that became the technical standard for modern kendo.

Itto-ryu has preserved a greater number of its derivative styles than any other school of kenjutsu and is today one of the most viable "families" of classical Japanese swordsmanship. There are six lines of Itto-ryu still being practiced today, with a sufficient number of exponents and level of skill to ensure that their art will be passed on intact to future generations: Ono-ha Itto-ryu, Mizoguchi-ha Itto-ryu, Nakanishi-ha Itto-ryu, Kogen Itto-ryu, Hokushin Itto-ryu, and Itto Shoden Muto-ryu.

THE DEVELOPMENT OF ITTO-RYU KENJUTSU

Itto-ryu kenjutsu was created during the late Sengoku jidai (Warring States period, 1467–1568) by a man named Ito Ittosai Kagehisa. At the age of thirteen, Ittosai is said to have floated on a piece of timber across the Bay of Sagami to the village of Ito, on the Izu Peninsula. He supposedly lived under the floor of a local shrine and practiced swordsmanship on his own. After repelling some bandits who had threatened the village, grateful residents gave him some money and one of the swords that had been dedicated to the shrine, enabling him to begin his search for proper instruction. He studied Chujo-ryu *tojutsu* (swordsmanship) with Kanemaki Jissai, a student of Toda Seigen, who was famous for his superlative short sword technique, and then embarked on *musha shugyo* (an itinerant warrior's journey, made for the purpose of testing or improving one's martial skills), traveling in the Kansai and Kanto regions.

During this "warrior journey," Ito had several experiences, when he spontaneously performed a movement under the stress of combat, that influenced his thinking about swordsmanship, and he later incorporated these insights into his system. The techniques he created, *zetsumyo ken* and *muso ken*, refer to the mystic, "ineffable," and "miraculous" nature of highly skilled swordsmanship, where trained actions take place without conscious thought. After further training and study, Ito combined the Chujo-ryu teachings with his own personal discoveries to create his own system of kenjutsu. He named it the Itto-ryu (One Sword Style), a reflection of his belief that the essence of swordsmanship could be stated in a simple phrase, *itto sunawachi banto*, "one sword [technique] gives rise to ten thousand sword [technique]s" which was in turn derived from an understanding of the underlying essentials of personal combat: *maai* (distancing), *hyoshi/choshi* (timing/rhythm), *hasuji* (literally, "blade line," trajectory and/or targeting), and *kurai* (mental and physical stance or preparedness).

GENERAL BACKGROUND
Ono-ha Itto-ryu

Ono-ha Itto-ryu is recognized as the senior line of the Itto-ryu styles of swordsmanship. It was founded by Ono Jiroemon Tadaaki, who succeeded Ito Ittosai Kagehisa as the second head of Itto-ryu kenjutsu.

An example of how the Ono-ha Itto-ryu shidachi (left) "cuts through"
uchidachi's attack and controls the center line

Originally, his name was Mikogami Tenzen, and Ono was the name he took after becoming the head of the school.

After Tadaaki was appointed *kenjutsu shinan-yaku* (instructor in swordsmanship) to Ieyasu's son, the second Tokugawa shogun, Tokugawa Hidetada, Itto-ryu became one of two official kenjutsu schools of the Tokugawa shogunate. He also served Iemitsu, the third shogun, in this capacity.

The fourth headmaster, Tadakazu, instructed the lord of the Tsugaru *han* (domain, in present-day Aomori Prefecture), Tsugaru Echigo-no-kami Nobumasa, in the entire system of the Ono-ha Itto-ryu and established a separate Tsugaru line. Other feudal lords and senior retainers throughout Japan also studied the ryu, and this served to increase its reputation and prestige in both the capital and provincial castle towns.

Tsugaru Tosa-no-kami Nobutoshi, second lord of Tsugaru, returned the transmission to the Ono family when he instructed both Ono Tadahisa (who died soon after) and Tadakata. After this time, both the Ono and the Tsugaru families transmitted the main, or orthodox, line of Ono-ha Itto-ryu.

In the Kansei period (1789–1801), the seventh head of the school, Ono Tadayoshi, taught a Tsugaru retainer by the name of Yamaga Hachirozaemon Takami the entire Ono-ha Itto-ryu curriculum and after that, the Tsugaru and Yamaga families worked together to transmit the system. This semi-formal collaboration continued until the Taisho period (1912–1926), when Sasamori Junzo, a well-known kendoist, Christian minister, and educator, who later became an influential politician noted for his work for international peace, inherited the ryu. The seventeenth generation headmaster, active today, is Junzo's son, Takemi, also an ordained minister and prominent educator. Ono-ha Itto-ryu is also practiced independently, outside the purview of the mainline of the ryu, by kendo teachers and exponents throughout Japan, and is thus probably the most widely disseminated form of Itto-ryu today.

Mizoguchi-ha Itto-ryu

The founder of Mizoguchi-ha Itto-ryu kenjutsu was a man named Mizoguchi Shingoemon Masakatsu. He had studied with Ono Jiroemon Tadatsune, the second head of Ono-ha Itto-ryu, before creating his own style. In the middle of the Edo period (1600–1868), a student of Mizoguchi's named Ito Masamori visited the Aizu han (in present-day Fukushima Prefecture), where he taught one of the clan retainers, Edamatsu Kimitada. Masamori, however, left before teaching the entire system to Edamatsu.

Edamatsu, in turn, taught Ikegami Jozaemon Yasumichi, who later went to Edo (present-day Tokyo) on his daimyo's orders to continue his training in swordsmanship. Ikegami studied not only Mizoguchi-ha

The cutting movement that follows shidachi's opening movement to uchidachi's left side. Shidachi has used the force of uchidachi's thrust to turn around the axis of the attack.

Itto-ryu, but other kenjutsu styles as well, though it is not recorded which styles these were. Later, with more training and experience, Ikegami incorporated his ideas and experience in Mizoguchi-ha Itto-ryu and other systems and founded his own variation of the system; this then became the Aizu line of Mizoguchi-ha Itto-ryu kenjutsu, which was passed down to warriors of the domain. Because of the partial nature of the original transmission, and subsequent developments in the art as it was practiced in the Aizu-Wakamatsu area, there are said to be significant differences between Mizoguchi's original art and that practiced by swordsmen of the Aizu han. The original line of the ryu has long been lost, however, so it is difficult to tell just what these differences are. Presently, the Fukushima prefectural and local kendo federations are responsible for practicing and transmitting the art to future generations.

Nakanishi-ha Itto-ryu

Nakanishi-ha Itto-ryu is probably closer to Ono-ha Itto-ryu, from which it is derived, than any other branch of Itto-ryu kenjutsu. The founder, Nakanishi Chuta Tanesada, studied with either the fifth generation headmaster of Ono-ha Itto-ryu, Ono Jiroemon Tadakata, or Ono Jiroemon Tadakazu, the sixth headmaster,[1] and then left to establish his own style, which he named after himself (*-ha* meaning faction or school). His son, Nakanishi Chuzo Tanetake, succeeded him and introduced the use of *bogu* (protective equipment) and *shinai* (bamboo swords) in regular practice. Other schools of kenjutsu, notably Shinkage-ryu, Nen-ryu, and Tatsumi-ryu used a slightly different type of bamboo training sword in order to prevent or reduce injuries, but the equipment introduced by Tanetake led to the Nakanishi-ha's rapid popularization, as it allowed exponents to train more freely and to engage in free-style matches resembling the competitive sport-form of modern kendo.

Over the years, many famous swordsmen have come from Nakanishi-ha Itto-ryu, some of them going on to establish ryu of their own. Among them are such notable warriors as Terada Gouemon (founder of Tenshin Itto-ryu), Shirai Toru (Terada's successor), Takayanagi Matashiro Toshitatsu (or Yoshimasa, the founder of Takayanagi-ha Toda-ryu), Asari Yoshinobu (the teacher of Yamaoka Tesshu), and Chiba Shusaku (founder of Hokushin Itto-ryu). More recently, the Meiji-period headmaster of Nakanishi-ha Itto-ryu, Takano Sazaburo Toyomasa, a prominent educator, worked to develop both the technical and philosophical aspects of the modern art of swordsmanship and establish it in the public school system. He was also one of the men instrumental in refining the Nihon Kendo Kata, and he helped to find a place for kendo in modern society.

Kogen Itto-ryu

Kogen Itto-ryu kenjutsu is perhaps most famous as the ryu studied by the mad swordsman in the novel and film titled *Daibosatsu Toge* (the English title is "Sword of Doom"). It is an amalgamation of the household martial traditions of the Henmi family and Mizoguchi-ha

Itto-ryu. Kogen Itto-ryu was founded by Henmi Tashiro Yoshitoshi, a descendant of a branch of the Takeda family, who are themselves descended from the Emperor Seiwa through Minamoto no Tsunemoto and Shinrasaburo Minamoto no Yoshimitsu (also in the lineage of Daito-ryu aikijujutsu). The name of the ryu is derived by combining the first character of Kai province, where the Takeda family lived (in present-day Yamanashi Prefecture; the character is pronounced "ko"), with that of their ancestral family (Minamoto is one of the most prestigious names to have in one's lineage; pronounced "gen"), and an acknowledgment of the Itto-ryu's contribution to this school of swordsmanship.

Kogen Itto-ryu developed as a discrete style of kenjutsu when an exponent of the Aizu Mizoguchi-ha Itto-ryu, Sakurai Gosuke Nagamasa, came to the Chichibu area (present-day Saitama Prefecture) and taught Henmi Yoshitoshi the techniques of his style. Sakurai came to acknowledge the technical superiority of his erstwhile student by later becoming a disciple of the Kogen Itto-ryu, accepting Henmi as his teacher. He stayed with the Henmi family for years, was cared for by them in his old age, and is buried in the Henmi family cemetery near their home.

The Henmi family was well known as a family of strong swordsmen, but they were not retainers of a particular lord and did not serve or live in a *joka machi* (castle town). The family farmed its own land and taught people who came to the area for instruction. Students generally trained in the morning and evening, and worked in the fields during the afternoon, trading their labor for tuition.

The dojo is in a typical old-style *nagaya* (long building) to the front of their house, where the Henmis established the Yobukan Dojo, which became famous throughout the province. Farming equipment is kept in a number of small storage rooms on the left as one goes through the gate; the dojo is to the right.

The current dojo was built more than two hundred years ago by the founder and is not a terribly large space, perhaps fifteen meters long and five meters wide. An old *kago* (palanquin) is kept up in the rafters. Old farming equipment (some of it for silkworm cultivation) is also

Entrance to the Yobukan Dojo at the Henmi family home
in Saitama Prefecture

stored there. A large door leads in from the earthen courtyard. As one looks toward the "front" of the dojo, there is a small raised *shihan shitsu* (room for the teachers) off to the left, covered with straw mats; in that room is an image of Marishiten, to which members of the dojo bow at the beginning and end of training. A couple of spears and naginata, used for special demonstrations, are kept over the door of the shihan shitsu; otherwise, trainees bring their own equipment with them and nothing is left at the dojo. Currently, Henmi Chifuji serves as the ninth headmaster of the ryu.

Hokushin Itto-ryu

The Hokushin Itto-ryu was founded by Chiba Shusaku Narimasa, one of the most famous swordsmen of the late Edo period. He originally studied his family's martial art, the Hokushin Muso-ryu, and later studied Itto-ryu kenjutsu with Nakanishi Chubei Tanetada and Asari Matashichiro Yoshinobu. After undergoing years of training, he traveled around the country, studying the strong points of different schools and incorporating them into his own art. Chiba founded his own style when he came to believe traditional Itto-ryu techniques and training methods he had learned in the Asari and Nakanishi dojo lacked essential elements. In naming his school, he honored both his family tradition and the Itto-ryu that formed the core of his training by calling it the Hokushin Itto-ryu.

The Gembukan Dojo that Chiba opened in the Kanda area was one of the largest in nineteenth-century Edo, and Hokushin Itto-ryu became one of the most representative schools of the time, along with Jikishinkage-ryu, Kyoshin Meichi-ryu, Shingyoto-ryu, and Shinto Munen-ryu. It was located just around the corner from the Tenjin Shinyo-ryu jujutsu dojo of Iso Mataemon Masatari; the men were good friends and co-operated closely, and many of their trainees belonged to both dojo.

The ryu was also very closely allied with the Tokugawa family of Mito as an official school of the domain. It had become affiliated with Shin Tamiya-ryu iaijutsu which was also taught there; today the two schools are being taught at the Mito Tobukan Dojo, one of the premier training venues for kendo in the Kanto area, under the direction of the Kozawa family.

Itto Shoden Muto-ryu

Yamaoka Tetsutaro Takayuki, more commonly known as Tesshu, was one of the most remarkable swordsmen of the nineteenth century. Indeed, his place is probably assured among the greatest swordsmen of Japanese history, even though he never used his sword in anger. A devotee of Zen, an accomplished artist and calligrapher, he studied a number of ryu over the years, most notably Ono-ha Itto-ryu and Nakanishi-ha Itto-ryu. Tesshu, in fact, received the full transmissions of both the Nakanishi line and the Ono-ha Itto-ryu from their respective headmasters. In creating his own line of transmission, he named it the Itto Shoden Muto-ryu to emphasize that he was passing on the correct transmission of Itto-ryu principles and techniques. The term "Muto" (No-Sword) refers to the realization that Yamaoka attained through years of meditation that the difference between Sword and Self, and between oneself and one's opponent is illusory and that the

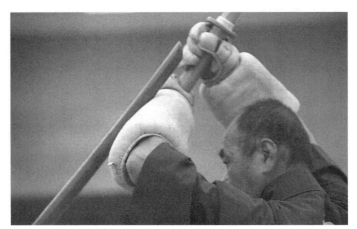

The final cut in an Ono-ha Itto-ryu kata,
with a close look at the onigote worn by uchidachi

underlying unity of all is the most important thing in swordsmanship. Today, there are very few exponents of Yamaoka's school, most likely because its training methods are so severe. It is now practiced in Kanazawa Prefecture, on the Japan Sea side of Japan. Murakami Yasumasa, who learned from a late Chief Justice of the Supreme Court, Ishida Kazuto, is the sixth generation head of the school.

Distinguishing Characteristics
Ono-ha Itto-ryu

Ono-ha Itto-ryu kenjutsu has an extensive curriculum, with more than one hundred fifty techniques. Both the *odachi* (long sword) and *kodachi* (short sword) are studied in sets covering both theoretical and practical aspects of swordsmanship. All of the *waza* are *suhada kempo* (unarmored swordsmanship), although they can be easily adapted to techniques done in armor (*kaisha kempo*).

The central principle of Itto-ryu kenjutsu is expressed in the phrase *itto sunawachi banto,* "one sword is ten thousand swords"; that is, if one understands swordsmanship's fundamental principles, one technique embodies and informs all other techniques and situations a swordsman

118

might encounter. The signature waza of the Itto-ryu is *kiriotoshi*,[2] which entails allowing the opponent to attack at will. The Itto-ryu exponent waits for the attack to develop, then cuts straight through the center of the enemy's body and attacking motion, overriding his sword and disrupting the attack before it can be completed. Many, perhaps most, of the techniques end with a full-impact cut to the wrists or forearms, which are raised in the *jodan* position. To withstand the force of this final blow, the *uchidachi* (the individual acting as the attacker) wears a special pair of articulated deerhide gauntlets that are very thickly padded. These are known as *onigote* and are one of the distinguishing characteristics of the Itto-ryu lines; all but two include their use in training.

Mizoguchi-ha Itto-ryu

Mizoguchi-ha Itto-ryu technique is notable for its *sayu tenka demi no hitachi*, a set of five odachi and three kodachi techniques characterized by the use of very smooth and adroit movements to both the left and right sides of the opponent's attack, followed by an immediate cutting or thrusting counter-movement. *Zanshin* (a state of intense awareness and concentration) is intense, starting with the initial movement of the exponents from *toma* (a "far-away" distance, generally about three to five paces away from one another) to *kosa* (literally "crossing," with the swords crossing at the *monouchi* or "working area" of the blade, about 15 cm. from the tip). At this point, uchidachi presses *shidachi* (the individual performing the "winning" side of the technique), forcing him to back up. Shidachi then re-establishes a measure of control and returns to the center of the training area. Uchidachi then attacks with either a cutting or thrusting movement and forces shidachi to evade the attack to either the left or right. As uchidachi continues his attack, it is countered to one or another side. These techniques all demonstrate possible responses to both sides. It should be further noted that the odachi techniques have both *omote* (surface level) and *ura* (inner, more sophisticated level), and there are a number of variations, so the curriculum is actually larger than it appears at first glance.

Shidachi in hasso no kamae, is closing on a stationary uchidachi,
who is standing in seigan no kamae.

What is particularly noticeable about Mizoguchi-ha Itto-ryu swordsman is the smoothness of their techniques. Their lack of vocalized *kiai* is also evident: the waza are silent, but the stark intensity as uchidachi and shidachi close is literally breathtaking. Also, unlike most kenjutsu schools, whose weapons make sounds as they contact one another, swords of Mizoguchi-ha Itto-ryu exponents make almost no sound at all. There is, nonetheless, a very strong sensation of the swords' *cutting* and the attention paid to timing and to the line of the attack is beautiful in its severity. One gets a very distinct sense that there is no slack at all in their techniques and that facing a Mizoguchi-ha swordsman would have been a difficult thing, indeed.

Nakanishi-ha Itto-ryu

The basic Nakanishi-ha Itto-ryu *kata* are, at least superficially, essentially the same as those of its parent Ono-ha Itto-ryu. What differs are the more subtle aspects of timing, breathing, and use of distancing.

Naturally, other interpretations and variations have developed over time, but the differences are quite subtle and require that one observe both schools over a period of several years to detect and understand how the two schools have diverged.

The general impression one receives viewing Nakanishi-ha Itto-ryu is of power and dignity. The stances are wide, the movement is deliberate. Even when techniques are done rapidly they seem slow, due to the intensity and gravity displayed by the exponents in their practice. As in Ono-ha Itto-ryu, the uchidachi wears onigote, the heavy gauntlets that allow them to receive full-power strikes to the wrists and forearms at the end of the kata.

Kogen Itto-ryu

There are twenty-five sword techniques in Kogen Itto-ryu and five *naginata* waza, which were introduced from the Toda-ha Buko-ryu. That may not seem like a very large technical repertoire, but the content of the techniques is so well conceived and executed that any more would be extraneous.

Although the iaijutsu techniques are no longer practiced, their names remain in the mokuroku and deserve mention, because of their unusual nature. Unlike any other ryu that I've seen, the iai techniques are referred to by the various *kuji* (literally, "nine characters," derived from esoteric Buddhism, used by koryu in various ways to instill particular mental states that are useful in combat and in training). Each of the characters is associated with a particular Buddhist worthy, but detailed information about the techniques is not available. Most current members of the Kogen Itto-ryu are skilled exponents of Muso Shinden-ryu iaido and kendo, as well as the classical techniques; some also have backgrounds in jojutsu or other modern unarmed arts.

Kogen Itto-ryu technique is very spare, with an economy of movement and a very strict sense of "line" and "timing." It has no superfluous content, although the meaning or utility of some movements is not immediately apparent. The *reiho* (formal etiquette) of the ryu is also fairly unique and seems to be a development of the mid-Edo period in that a *tachiainin* (observer) lays out the weapons and stays in

*Shidachi, right, has deflected uchidachi's thrust and
counterattacked to uchidachi's left wrist and midsection.*

attendance throughout the performance of techniques, a holdover from dueling etiquette.[3]

Another holdover from the past is the presence of a number of Kogen Itto-ryu dojo throughout the area of what used to be called Musashi Province. Licensed instructors of the ryu taught in their own dojo and, over the years, different lines of teaching developed, leading to several minor differences in technique and even in curriculum. The headmaster of the ryu is still a member of the Henmi family and he continues to teach and train in the Yobukan Dojo; other people do the same in other parts of Saitama Prefecture. All, however, continue to maintain close contact with the Henmi family, "touching base with the source"; this has led to a remarkable vitality and a sense of camaraderie among the scattered students that will likely ensure that Kogen Itto-ryu will remain a vital part of their respective communities.

Hokushin Itto-ryu

Hokushin Itto-ryu was created late in the Tokugawa era; practice in the nineteenth century placed a heavy emphasis on *shinai geiko*, using the protective equipment and bamboo swords popularized by Nakanishi Tanetake, as well as the traditional kata. After more than two hundred fifty years of the enforced peace of *Pax Tokugawa*, and the subsequent lack of chances to apply their skills in combat, many members of the *bushi* class were no longer satisfied with practicing only kata. Moreover, the newly developed protective equipment made possible a type of vigorous training (known as *ji geiko* in modern kendo) that was attractive to young men of the period and helped the Hokushin Itto-ryu (and other schools that also placed an emphasis on this kind of study) gain many members.

When modern kendo was formally established during the mid-Meiji period (1868–1912), and its technical curriculum was being formed, several members of the committee responsible for this work were senior exponents of the Hokushin Itto-ryu. Because of their level of skill in this kind of freestyle practice, they exerted a great influence on both the techniques and training methods of modern Japanese kendo.

Hokushin Itto-ryu technique is predicated on the ability to continually press the opponent and, no matter how he tries to attack, to be able to "ride" his sword, cutting through and knocking it down in the kiriotoshi action, and especially to strike at the very instant the enemy attempts to attack.

The techniques are relatively simple in appearance, rather like those of Kogen Itto-ryu in that sense, with no waste or flashy movement. The uchidachi wears the same sort of onigote that are used in Ono-ha and Nakanishi-ha Itto-ryu kata. The stances appear to be slightly more erect than in other Itto-ryu systems, but the finishing techniques are delivered with the same feeling of weight and power. Indeed, the "gravity" of Hokushin Itto-ryu technique is striking and leaves a very strong impression, a sort of "after-image," on those who see it.

Itto Shoden Muto-ryu

Muto-ryu kata resemble, not surprisingly, those of its two parent Itto-ryu styles (Ono-ha and Nakanishi-ha), with what appears to be an admixture of elements from Jikishinkage-ryu, which Yamaoka is also said to have studied. There are over fifty techniques in the ryu's curriculum, similar to Itto-ryu in general, but done with a slightly different "flavor" than in either Ono-ha or Nakanishi-ha. As in those schools, the uchidachi wears the onigote; the *bokuto* (wooden swords) used are fairly straight and heavy. An unusual feature of some Itto Shoden Muto-ryu kata is the stance taken on one leg, which comes from Jikishinkage-ryu.[4]

CONCLUSION

All of the koryu kenjutsu ryu include distinctive, effective techniques that were developed and refined over generations and through the efforts of many extraordinary men. Though several classical systems of swordsmanship extant today are older than the various schools of the Itto-ryu tradition, Itto-ryu is considered one of the most truly representative forms of Japanese swordsmanship, due to its sophisticated theory and training methods and its influence on modern kendo, the Way of the Sword.

The "apparent" simplicity of Itto-ryu, relying as it does on "one technique [which becomes] ten thousand techniques," in accord with the most fundamental principles of combat, has provided a firm technical base. This template enables students of both classical and modern swordsmanship to learn and study the art in all its aspects. It is in large part due to the dedication and determination of past and present exponents of the Itto-ryu that this transmission has been maintained, and it is a debt that modern exponents must always keep in mind as they guide their ryu into this new millennium.

Notes

1 Both names appear in various sources; which headmaster Nakanishi studied with is unclear.
2 Interestingly, the other "official school" of the Tokugawa shogunate, Yagyu Shinkage-ryu, has a very similar concept and the central technique of the school is almost identical. *Gasshi uchi* is the name of the technique; the concept is expressed in the phrase *katsujinken*, "life-giving sword," meaning Shinkage exponents will allow an enemy to do whatever he wants, observe the situation closely, and then respond with the "correct" technique.
3 According to what a senior instructor told me.
4 There are very few people who study this system and it is seldom seen outside of Ishikawa Prefecture; thus, it is difficult to provide a more detailed technical description.

References

Japan: An Illustrated Encyclopedia. 1993. Tokyo: Kodansha.

Draeger, D.F. 1973B. *Classical Budo.* The Martial Arts and Ways of Japan, 2. New York & Tokyo: Weatherhill.

Draeger, D.F., and R.W. Smith. 1981. *Comprehensive Asian Fighting Arts.* Tokyo: Kodansha.

Kawauchi, T. 1954. *Kaicho Zoho: Nihon Budo Ryuso-den* (Traditions and Founders of the Japanese Martial Arts). Tokyo: Nihon Kobudo Shinkokai Jimukyoku.

Miyazaki, Y., ed. 1994. *Nihon Densho Bugei Ryuha: Dokuhon* (Japanese Martial Traditions: A Reader). Tokyo: Shin Jimbutsu Oraisha.

Nihon Kobudo Kyokai. 1984. Itto-ryu Nagare (The Lineage of the Itto-ryu). In *Seventh All-Japan Kobudo Embu Taikai Program.* Tokyo: Nippon Budokan.

Nihon Kobudo Kyokai. 1988. *Nihon Kobudo Sokan* (An Overview of the Japanese Classical Martial Arts). Tokyo: Shimazu Shobo.

Osano, J. 1994. *Zusetsu Nihon Bugei Bunka Gairon* (Illustrated Overview of Japanese Martial Art Culture). Tokyo: Fuyosha.

Papinot, E. 1972. *Historical and Geographical Dictionary of Japan.* Rutland, Vt. & Tokyo, Japan: Charles E. Tuttle Co.

Sakai, S. 1977. *Kogen Itto-ryu.* Chichibu, Saitama-ken: Self-published.

Sasama, Y. 1982. *Nihon Budo Jiten* (The Dictionary of Japanese Martial Arts). Tokyo: Kashiwa Shobo Ltd.

Sasamori, J. 1965. *Itto-ryu Gokui* (The Secret Teachings of the Itto-ryu). Tokyo: Itto-ryu Gokui Hankokai.

Shimokawa, U. 1925. *Kendo no Hattatsu* (The Development of Kendo). Kyoto: Dai Nippon Butokukai.

Skoss, M. 1976–1997. Personal notes and videotapes of *embu* (martial arts demonstrations) in various parts of Japan.

Takano, H. 1985. *Heiho Itto-ryu* (Itto-ryu Martial Strategies). Tokyo: Kodansha Ltd.

Tominaga, K. 1972. *Kendo Gohyakunen-shi* (A Five Hundred Year History of Kendo). Tokyo: Shiraizumi Shobo Ltd.

Watatani, K., and T. Yamada. 1983. *Bugei Ryuha Daijiten* (Dictionary of Japanese Martial Art Traditions). Tokyo: Tokyo Kopii Shuppanbu.

William M. Bodiford is an associate professor in the Department of East Asian Languages and Cultures at the University of California, Los Angeles (UCLA). He is the author of **Soto Zen in Medieval Japan** *(1994) as well as the entries "Religion and Spiritual Development: Japan" and "Written Texts: Japan" in* **Martial Arts of the World: An Encyclopedia** *(2001). Bodiford holds* **menkyo kaiden** *and* **shihan** *licenses in Kashima-Shinryu.*

SOKE
HISTORICAL INCARNATIONS OF
A TITLE AND ITS ENTITLEMENTS

William M. Bodiford

Who or what is a *soke*? If Internet websites can be believed, in the English-speaking world the Japanese word soke has become a title for individuals who claim to be "great grandmasters" or "founders" of martial arts.[1] Surprisingly, however, the term is not explained in recent English-language dictionaries of martial arts directed toward general readers, nor in the more authoritative books about Japanese martial culture.[2] Apparently this very obscurity provides commercial advantage when it is invoked in a competitive marketplace crowded with instructors who promote themselves not just as high-ranking black belts, but as masters or even grandmasters. This English-language usage stands in stark contrast to the connotations of the word soke in Japan where, if it is used at all, it strongly implies loyalty to existing schools, deference to ancestral authority, and conservative adherence to traditional forms. Despite what many seem to believe in the West, as a Japanese word soke has never meant "founder," nor does it mean "grandmaster."

Confusion over the word soke, however, is not confined to people who lack Japanese-language skills; it exists in Japan as well. These misunderstandings arise because in premodern and modern Japan the term represents different (yet related) meanings and connotations depending on the diverse contexts in which it appears. We can distinguish several different patterns of usage associated with the term soke throughout Japanese history.[3] For this reason, when describing soke in English (or, rather, when arguing about its meaning) it is useful first to chronicle the many ways that this word has been used in the historical record. Then one can better evaluate the ways that this term has been conceptualized by modern writers and applied (or misapplied) in contemporary situations.

Soke originated as a Chinese word (Mandarin *zongjia*) with strong familial and religious connotations. Etymologically it is written with glyphs indicating a family that performs ancestor rites. In Chinese texts it designates either the members of a household belonging to the same clan or the main lineage within an extended clan, the head of which was responsible for maintaining the ancestral temple on behalf of the entire clan organization. In Japanese texts as well, soke always implied a familial relationship replete with filial duties. Japanese use of this word was not limited to consanguineous contexts, though, since many kinds of social relationships were organized around pseudo-familial models. Religious societies, commercial enterprises, and teaching organizations all employed familial vocabulary and observed rites of familial etiquette. In these contexts, the term soke often implied exclusivity and commercial privilege, with less emphasis on formal religious duties.

For most of early Japanese history the privileges of power, wealth, and civilization were controlled exclusively by the court, the aristocrats, and the Buddhist clergy, all three of which reinforced one another in mutual dependence. As Buddhist clerics developed their combined exoteric-esoteric (*ken-mitsu*) form of tantra, they gave rise to a shared "culture of secret transmission" (Stone, 97–152). In other words, Buddhist pedagogical systems in which tantric rituals were taught via oral initiations (*kuden*) available only to members of exclusive master-disciple lineages became the normative teaching method across elite society (Nishiyama 1982B, 146–147). Within this culture, the arts of civilization prized most by wealthy nobles became the exclusive property of certain families. For example, the Nijo and Reizei branches of the aristocratic Fujiwara family each taught and maintained control over mutually exclusive systems of initiation into the mysteries of Japanese poetics (*waka*). Lower down on the economic ladder, designated merchant families exercised exclusive commercial control over the production and distribution of certain types of manufactured goods used by aristocrats, such as extravagant ceramics (for example, *raku* ware; Nishiyama

1982B, 51). Those families maintained their hereditary monopolies through the protection and patronage of local nobles or of the court.

These families operated much like corporate entities in which many affiliated kinship groups functioned in unison. Among the members of the united kinship groups only the individual successor — usually the oldest son — of the current family head received full initiation into the secrets of the family craft. Even if proper male progeny did not exist, economic necessity demanded that the main family line always continue since hereditary authority rested with that family alone. Whenever required, therefore, another male from one of the affiliated groups would be brought in and designated as heir to succeed the head of the family. The heir, whether related by blood or adopted, was responsible for maintaining the unity of the corporate families, maintaining their commercial monopoly, and maintaining their good relations with their patrons. Most of all he was responsible for preserving the secret texts, special tools, and knowledge of the oral initiations that constituted his family's exclusive lore. The legitimate possessors of that exclusive lore, both the main family itself as a multi-generational entity, and the individual current head of the family were called the soke. Use of this term was extremely limited, however, until after the establishment of the Tokugawa peace in 1603 provided the conditions for the development of new, more elaborate systems of familial privilege throughout the land.

During the Tokugawa period (1603–1868) of Japanese history, especially during the eighteenth century, many new types of artistic and cultural activities came under the domination of families that exercised proprietary authority over the performance of those arts and endeavors by others. These new familial lineages, which essentially operated as commercial guilds, referred to themselves as soke. The leading expert on this subject is a Japanese scholar named Nishiyama Matsunosuke. Early in his career, Nishiyama wrote two seminal studies of soke families and the ways they exercised their authority during this period of Japanese history: *Iemoto monogatari* (Iemoto Stories, 1956; reprinted as Nishiyama 1982A) and *Iemoto no kenkyu* (Researches in the Iemoto System, 1960; reprinted as Nishiyama 1982B).[4] Although Nishiyama settled on the term *iemoto*, in the Tokugawa-period texts he studied the words iemoto and soke were used interchangeably, without any distinction in meaning (Nishiyama 1982B, 15). Both words were used to refer to the main lineage that asserted proprietary authority over a commercial guild or to refer to the person who had attained full initiation as the current legitimate head of that lineage.

Nishiyama cites several factors that contributed to the development of familial lineages (i.e., soke) as commercial guilds. The Tokugawa regime placed governmental authority in the hands of an upper echelon of warrior families who maintained their positions of power through assertions of hereditary privilege and attempts to enforce rigid codes of social distinctions. These new warrior elites readily accepted similar assertions of familial authority over the codification and teaching of artistic endeavors (Nishiyama 1982B, 91–92). Moreover, the warrior rulers patronized many new performative arts and forms of amusement that had developed independently from and, thus, outside the control of the old aristocratic families. It was the teachers of these new amusements — arts such as tea ceremony (*chanoyu*), flower arranging (*ikebana*), chess (*shogi*), Noh theater, verse (*haikai*), special forms of music and dance, and so forth — that most quickly asserted familial control over their teaching and over their performance by others (Nishiyama 1982B, 135–140). Finally, the long period of peace produced many unemployed former warriors (*ronin*) who could seek employment as junior instructors in these guilds; at the same time, the end of incessant warfare promoted the economic prosperity that enabled townsmen and rural landowners to amass surplus wealth that they could spend as pupils of these arts.

The existence of a network of junior instructors (i.e., *natori*) who taught in the name of the soke is a crucial feature that distinguished Tokugawa-period soke families from their earlier counterparts (Nishiyama 1982B, 106). During the Tokugawa period, instruction in the special skills associated with a particular artistic endeavor was marketed through networks of branch instructors who paid royalties and license fees to the soke and who were organized into a pyramid-like hierarchical structure with the soke on top. The soke asserted absolute authority over the branch instructors and indirect authority over their students by controlling what, how, and when subjects could be taught and by restricting access to the most advanced lore, to which the soke alone was privy. Nishiyama labeled the social structures associated with this type of exclusive familial control and networks of branch instructors the iemoto system (*iemoto seido*). He saw it as a unique feature of Japanese feudalism that exerted a strong influence over the development of many traditional Japanese arts even until modern times (Nishiyama 1982B, 20–21).

These Tokugawa-period artistic lineages can be likened to commercial guilds because they earned money from every single person who participated in their particular school's craft or art throughout the entire country. Nishiyama (1982B, 16) neatly summarizes the commercial rights (*kenri*) of these familial guilds as follows:

    1. Rights regarding the techniques (*waza*) of the art, such as the right to keep it secret, the right to control how and when it is performed, and rights over the repertoire of its curriculum and its choreography (*kata*).

    2. Rights over instructors (*kyoju*), over initiation rituals and documents (*soden*), and over the awarding of diplomas and licenses (*menkyo*).

    3. The right to punish (*chobatsu*) and to expel (*hamon*) students.

    4. The right to control uses of costumes, of stage names or artistic pseudonyms, and so forth.

    5. The right to control facilities and special equipment or tools used in the art.

    6. Exclusive rights to the monetary income and social status resulting from the preceding five items.

For almost every art or amusement patronized by the ruling elite, there existed only a limited number of these familial guilds, each one of which enforced the above rights over anyone who practiced that art throughout the entire kingdom.[5] No one could legally perform a play, a song, a musical piece, or practice any other art in public without either joining the soke's school or paying fees for temporary permission (*ichinichi soden*). Enforcement of these exclusive rights enabled soke families to control huge populations of students across all strata of society. Nishiyama argues that from the middle of the eighteenth century these guilds provided a government-regulated medium for the distribution of cultural knowledge within which people assigned to different social classes (samurai of various ranks, townsmen, merchants, priests, wealthy farmers, rural warriors, etc.) could interact with one another on a near-equal footing (Nishiyama 1982B, 531; 1997, 204–208).

Nishiyama's research demonstrates that the near-monopoly control over the teaching of peaceful arts exercised by Tokugawa-period soke effectively prevented the proliferation of rival schools. In short, where soke existed, there were no new schools. The very creation of new schools repudiated any notion of soke authority (Nishiyama 1982B, 135–137). Seen in this light, it is obvious that the word soke in premodern Japanese documents could never be translated into English as "founder." The notion of "founder" is even less appropriate in modern Japan.

After 1868, when Japan became organized as a modern state, the government formally recognized the legal rights of soke (a.k.a. iemoto) families to control the copyright of all musical scores, theatrical plays, textbooks, and artistic works produced by members of their guilds (Nishiyama 1982B, 16). In this way, the terms soke and iemoto acquired legal definitions as designations for the modern representatives of the limited number of families who could provide historical documentation that they had controlled these kinds of commercial guilds during the Tokugawa period. To maintain their copyrights, the leaders of these families had to register with the government as legal entities. At the same time that they acquired copyrights, they lost their previous ability to restrict the teaching or performance of their arts by people from outside their guild. They became just one school or performance group among many. While they can restrict unauthorized use of their own name and their own historical resources, they have no legal power to inhibit competition. Today, as long as there is no copyright infringement, anyone can write new instructional guides to tea ceremony or

KEIKO SHOKON

any other traditional art. Anyone is free to devise new methods for practicing them.

Use of the term soke (or iemoto) in martial contexts is even more complex. Before 1868, soke families that were organized into the kinds of commercial guilds described above never controlled instruction in martial arts. This is the reason so many different lineages (*ryuha*) of martial arts existed in premodern Japan. The contrast between teaching organizations devoted to peaceful arts (such as tea ceremony, flower arranging, and so forth) and those concerned with martial arts could not be more stark. Instruction in any of the peaceful arts was available only from a small number of familial lineages, each one of which organized itself into a commercial guild with a network of affiliated branch instructors available throughout the land. On the other hand, there existed hundreds of different martial art lineages, the vast majority of which were confined to a single location.[6] While many martial lineages were consanguineous (i.e., handed down from father to son), many others were not.

Nishiyama (1982B, 273–278) identifies several reasons why martial art lineages never developed into iemoto (a.k.a. soke) systems. Prior to the establishment of the Tokugawa peace, rapid acquisition of military prowess constituted the sine qua non of any system of martial instruction. An instructor who withheld instruction in the most advanced techniques as a family secret, as was the norm among soke who taught peaceful arts, could not have attracted students. For this reason, during the sixteenth century, military students usually attained full initiation rather quickly, after which they were free to teach all that they had learned to their own students. If anyone issued diplomas, they did so on their own authority, without having to pay license fees to any larger organization. After the Tokugawa regime imposed peace on the land, both older and new schools of martial instruction became more structured, more secretive, and developed more complex and time-consuming curriculums. Students who received diplomas no longer necessarily acquired independent rights to issue diplomas themselves.[7] The ruling authorities also actively prevented any warrior groups or martial schools from developing organizational bonds across domain boundaries.[8]

Soke

Moreover, the rulers of each individual domain preferred to patronize only their own local martial systems, which could be kept under their own local control. Finally, in an age of peace it became practically impossible for any one martial lineage or group of lineages to demonstrate decisively their superiority over their rivals. Innovative teachers could (and did) devise new methods of martial training and establish new schools without having to risk lives to demonstrate their combat effectiveness.

Osano Jun (187–192) argues that the first marital art in Japan to adopt a true soke system was the Kodokan School of judo. Osano could be right. The Kodokan set the standards not just for members within one training hall in one location, but for all participants in judo throughout the nation. The Kodokan defined the art; it controlled licensing and instruction; and it established branch schools with instructors who maintained permanent affiliation with the headquarters. If the Kodokan does not recognize something as being "judo," then it is not judo. Therefore, there is no such thing as a new style of judo. All of these elements constitute essential characteristics of traditional soke organizations in Tokugawa-period Japan. In actual practice, however, no one ever refers to the Kodokan, or its current head, as the soke of judo.[9] The term seems out of place with judo's emphasis on modernity. Having analyzing the term soke in this way, Osano also criticizes the present-day use of the soke label by some Japanese teachers who represent traditional martial art lineages (i.e., *koryu*). Osano asserts that such usage not only is incorrect but also reveals an ignorance of traditional Japanese culture.

Osano's strict historical understanding is probably too strict. He overlooks the legal and social changes in the status of soke that occurred after 1868. After Japan began to modernize, social critics denounced soke organizations as a disagreeable legacy of a feudal system based on hereditary privilege, which stifled innovation and restricted knowledge for the financial benefit of undeserving family heads who no longer possessed the skills of their ancestors (Nishiyama 1982c, 263–273). Soke organizations saw their networks of branch instructors wither as interest in traditional arts declined and former students broke

136   KEIKO SHOKON

away to found rival schools.[10] Soon many traditional soke disappeared, especially in arts based on direct competition among participants such as Japanese chess (shogi) and in less well-known forms of dance and song. As more and more of these intangible cultural legacies disappeared, modern Japanese gradually developed a new appreciation for the soke families who had managed to preserve their own family traditions and teach them to new generations. Without the determination and persistence of the heirs of these families, direct knowledge of many traditional Japanese arts would have been lost.

Today one could argue that the historical differences between the heirs of Tokugawa-period family lineages which operated as commercial guilds (with the natori system) and the heirs of localized teaching lineages such as those associated with martial traditions are less significant than their modern similarities. In both cases the current successors remain the only legitimate sources for traditional forms of instruction in the arts of that lineage. In both cases the current successors have assumed responsibility for preserving the historical texts, special tools, unique skills, and specific lore that have been handed down within their own particular lineage. In both cases the current successors distinguish their traditional teachings from newly founded rivals by pointing out how their teachings remain faithful to the goals and forms taught by previous generations. Based on these similarities, many modern writers use the terms iemoto or soke as designations for the legitimate heir to any established main lineage. Used in reference to present-day representatives of traditional martial art lineages, therefore, the soke label properly denotes their roles as successors to and preservers of a particular historical and cultural legacy. It should not be interpreted as implying identification with a commercial network (as criticized by Osano) nor as being equivalent to "grandmaster" or "founder" (as mistakenly assumed by casual observers), and might best be translated simply as "head" or "headmaster."

Consider, for example, the case of Kashima-Shinryu (see Friday, *Legacies of the Sword*). In his books and articles, Seki Humitake, the current head of and nineteenth-generation successor to the Kashima-Shinryu lineage, uses the label soke as a designation for the Kunii family. He uses this term as a way of honoring the role the Kunii family played in preserving Kashima-Shinryu traditions. Down to the time of Seki's teacher, Kunii Zen'ya (1894–1966), Kashima-Shinryu forms of martial lore had been passed down consanguineously within the Kunii family from father to son from one generation to the next. Seki's modern use of the label soke simply acknowledges that legacy.[11] In the writings of Kunii Zen'ya and in the traditional scrolls preserved within the Kunii family, however, the word soke cannot be found. Kunii Zen'ya never referred to himself or to his family as the soke of Kashima-Shinryu. He simply signed his name. In writing out copies of his family's old scrolls (these copies would be handed out as diplomas), though, he usually would add the words "Kunii-ke soden" before the title of each scroll. For example, if he copied an old scroll titled "Kenjutsu mokuroku" he would give it the title "Kunii-ke soden kenjutsu mokuroku." In this example, the original title simply means "fencing curriculum" while the longer version means "the fencing curriculum transmitted within the Kunii family." Used to represent this sense of "transmitted within a family," the term soke seems perfectly reasonable. It merely implies that the lore associated with this curriculum was taught exclusively within the Kunii familial lineage.

In concluding, it is difficult to condone the use of obscure Japanese terminology to describe American social practices for which perfectly acceptable English words already exist. One must struggle to imagine how any non-Japanese could call himself a "soke" in English except as a joke. At the same time it is also difficult to regard this term with any special reverence or to become overly troubled by its misuse among self-proclaimed "grandmasters" and "founders." During the Tokugawa period the word soke designated a commercial system of hereditary privilege that took advantage of the ignorance of ordinary people for financial gain. Perhaps teachers of commercial martial art schools in America who adopt the title soke for themselves are more historically accurate in their usage than they themselves realize.

KEIKO SHOKON

Notes

This essay evolved in response to questions about the meaning of the term soke posted on the Internet website E-Budo.com (http://www.e-budo.com/). I wish to thank the many contributors to that discussion, especially Karl Friday, Toby Threadgill, and Robert Reinberger, for raising issues that helped me clarify my initial comments. I also wish to thank Diane Skoss of Koryu Books for providing me with this opportunity to revise my comments into an essay directed toward a larger audience.

1   Random examples of organizations with websites on the Internet (as of March 2002) that promote use of the word soke as a exalted martial art title include the following: (1) the World Head of Family Sokeship Council (http://www.bushido.org/~whfsc/whfsc.html), which boasts "the most elite and prestigious grandmasters council in the world"; (2) the World Sokeship Council (renamed to World Headfounders/Headfamilies Council in 1989; http://www.geocities.com/Tokyo/6471/), which states that it "was established to create a trully [*sic*] 'elite' and very prestigious fellowship or peer group for that very small group of martial artists who have achieved the right to be called a 'grandmaster' by their peers"; (3) Juko-Kai International (http://www.jukokai.com), which under a link titled "Soke's Corner" describes its own "Zen Kokusai Soke Budo/Bugei Renmei" (a.k.a., Zen Kokusai Soke Remmei [*sic*]) as the West's first recognized sokeship commission (founded 1970) and identifies soke as someone who founds his own martial art "ryu." I thank Jim Kass for informing me of these websites.

2   I could not find the word soke in Kim's popular dictionary, in Draeger's pioneering three-volume opus, nor in Hurst's scholarly history. In Frederic's dictionary it appears misspelled as *sokei* and is not defined but is mistakenly cross-referenced with *shodai*, which in turn is glossed as a title for the founder of a martial art "ryu" (i.e., ryuha or lineage).

3 In addition to its historical meanings, this word acquires additional implications when used by modern writers or cultural critics as an analytical concept to explain certain features of the social and historical contexts in which soke appears. (For an explanation of the difference between terms and concepts, see Hall 1983.)

4 For a brief English-language summary of his research, see the translator's introduction, pages 4–5, to Nishiyama 1997.

5 Nishiyama (1982B, 14, 19–20) cites *Shoryu Iemoto Kagami* (Directory of Iemoto Schools), a woodblock text printed sometime in the early nineteenth century, to provide some indication of the number and kinds of artistic schools (ryuha; i.e., commercial guilds) then existing in Japan. According to this text the ratios between arts and number of schools was as follows: abacus = 7 schools; flower arranging = 2 schools; tea ceremony = 1 school (the Senke) with 14 sub-divisions; incense = 2 schools; Noh = 6 schools; poetics (*waka*) = 2 schools; linked verse (*renga*) = 3 schools; minimal verse (*haikai*) = 6 schools; checkers (*go*) = 4 schools; chess (*shogi*) = 4 schools; wind pipes (*sho*) = 4 schools; horizontal flute (*fue*) = 3 schools; lute (*biwa*) = 4 schools; zither (*koto*) = 1 school; and so forth.

6 Nishiyama (1982B, 279) cites the research of Imamura Yoshio (subsequently published in 1967), which shows that during the nineteenth century more than seventy-one percent of the martial art schools listed in domain records were taught only in one location.

7 During the Tokugawa period instructors of all types, whether affiliated with an iemoto system (i.e., commercial guild), a martial lineage, or a religious institution, charged monetary fees for diplomas. To protect their interests, they severely restricted the rights of students to reveal what they had learned to outsiders without proper authorization. In martial lineages, new students customarily signed oaths of secrecy and advanced students pledged that upon their own deaths all scrolls, texts, and diplomas they had received would be returned to their instructor's household. There is no evidence, though, that these kinds of restrictions were observed by military students prior to the Tokugawa period.

8   Friday (18) and Hurst (178–179) also point out how government policies prevented martial art lineages from developing into iemoto systems.

9   Nishiyama (1982c, 291–292) also discusses the Kodokan as a social institution that rationalized and modernized many features of the premodern iemoto system.

10 The traditional soke schools of tea ceremony and flower arranging constitute the main exceptions to this trend. They have flourished by redefining themselves as institutions for promoting an appreciation for traditional Japanese culture and, especially, for teaching traditional values and etiquette to young women.

11 Friday (32, 49–50) also uses the label soke as a designation for the Kunii family, but based on his analysis of soke as lineages characterized by "proprietorship over a package of teachings vested exclusively in the hands of one individual per generation." Friday's usage emphasizes the conceptual similarity among all kinds of instructional lineages before, during, and after the Tokugawa period. In his view, the development of iemoto systems (i.e., networks of branch instructors) by lineages that taught peaceful arts merely constitutes an extreme commercialization across borders of the same rights of proprietorship exercised on a local level by martial lineages.

References

Draeger, D.F. 1973–1974. *The Martial Arts and Ways of Japan*. 3 volumes. New York & Tokyo: Weatherhill.

Friday, K.F., with H. Seki. 1997. *Legacies of the Sword: the Kashima-Shinryu and Samurai Martial Culture*. Honolulu: University of Hawai'i Press.

Hall, J.W. 1983. Terms and Concepts in Japanese History: An Inquiry into the Problems of Translation. *Journal of Japanese Studies* 9, no. 1: 1–32.

Hurst, G.C. 1998. *Armed Martial Arts of Japan: Swordsmanship and Archery*. New Haven: Yale University Press.

Imamura, Y. 1967. *Jukyuseiki ni Okeru Nihon Taiiku no Kenkyu* (Studies in Ninteenth-century Japanese Physical Education). Tokyo: Fumaido Shoten.

Kim, S.-J., D. Kogan, N. Kontogiannis, and H. Wong. 1995. *Tuttle Dictionary of the Martial Arts of Korea, China & Japan*. Rutland, VT: Charles E. Tuttle.

Louis, F. 1995. (1988) *A Dictionary of the Martial Arts* (Dictionnaire des Arts Martiaux). Translated and edited by P.H. Crompton. Rutland, VT: Charles E. Tuttle Co.

Nishiyama, M. 1982A (1956). *Iemoto Monogatari* (Iemoto Stories). Reprinted in *Iemotosei no Tenkai* (Development of the Iemoto System), vol. 2 of *Nishiyama Matsunosuke Chosakushu* (Collected Works). Tokyo: Yoshikawa Kobunkan.

———. 1982B (1960). *Iemoto no Kenkyu* (Researches in the Iemoto System). Reprinted as vol. 1 of *Nishiyama Matsunosuke Chosakushu* (Collected Works). Tokyo: Yoshikawa Kobunkan.

———. 1982C (1962). *Gendai no Iemoto* (Contemporary Iemoto). Reprinted in *Iemotosei No Tenkai* (Development of the Iemoto System), vol. 2 of *Nishiyama Matsunosuke Chosakushu* (Collected Works). Tokyo: Yoshikawa Kobunkan.

———. 1997. *Edo Culture Daily Life and Diversions in Urban Japan, 1600–1868*. Translated and edited by G. Groemer. Honolulu, HI: University of Hawai'i Press.

Osano, J. 1994. *Zusetsu Nihon Bugei Bunka Gairon* (Illustrated Overview of Japanese Martial Culture). Tokyo: Fuyosha.

Stone, J.I. 1999. *Original Enlightenment and the Transformation of Medieval Japanese Buddhism*. Honolulu: University of Hawai'i Press.

*Ellis Amdur has been teaching Japanese classical martial arts in Seattle since 1989. He holds a **shihan** license and the **okuden mokuroku** in Toda-ha Buko-ryu, and is licensed as **inkajo** in Araki-ryu. He is also the author of **Dueling with O-sensei: Grappling with the Myth of the Warrior Sage** (2000), a collection of his **Aikido Journal** essays, and **Old School: Essays on Japanese Martial Traditions** (2002). His company, Edgework, provides training in conflict resolution techniques; his website, http://www.ellisamdur.com/, features information on this training and his writings.*

RENOVATION AND INNOVATION IN TRADITION

Ellis Amdur

INTRODUCTION

Authorities have tended to present the martial *ryu* as if they were life encased in amber — pristine jewels suspended unchanged for hundreds of years. This is partly a problem of language. *Koryu*, according to Nelson's *Japanese-English Character Dictionary*, means, "old manners, old style, old school (of art)." But it goes against common sense that when koryu were young they were called "old." To the best of my knowledge, the general term for these systems of combat, in the period of their actual use, was *bugei* (the arts of war). This word, at least, has no nuance that one is preserving things unchanged.

The arts of war display a dynamic tension between innovation and tradition in every culture. When it comes to the battlefield, the conservative wing almost always loses, as Takeda Katsuyori's cavalry found at Nobunaga's muzzle points at Nagashino. There may have been soldiers who lamented the shift from earlier rifles to the M-16, particularly due to the latter's notorious propensity to jam, but there is no traditional wing in the Marines maintaining battalions armed with M-1s or better yet, muskets. On the other hand, anachronistic traditions such as the cavalry units maintained within the United States Army and the U.S. Coast Guard's square-rigged barque, the "Eagle," provide a vital link to a glorious past. There is no doubt that living traditions excite both the imagination and the spirit, creating an esprit de corps that is a powerful force. Consider the shiver that goes up one's spine at the eerie sound of the bagpipes or *horagai*,[1] or the way the blood throbs in one's chest at the sound of military drummers.

Many cultures have maintained combative traditions over time. Most often, however, these concern fighting arts as methods of combat or ritual within a civil society — not ways of going to war. The martial ryu are quite unusual, in that outmoded methods of warfare have been maintained for many generations. Perhaps the primary reasons for this was the Tokugawa shogunate's imposition of two hundred and fifty some years of totalitarian peace. With no external threats, with competing feudal lords politically neutralized and farmer's revolts easily put down with musketry, there was no need for either tactical or technological innovation. Once combative arts were confined within a caste structure, the access to weaponry limited, and new technology largely circumscribed, conservatism actually aided totalitarian rule.

A TRADITION OF INNOVATION

That we don't see the innovative side of Japanese martial traditions is, I believe, because we see the trees instead of the forest. There are lots of "old-growth" trees anyway — those that exemplify the conservative wing described above. But a closer look will reveal that, although individual ryu may have changed little, Japanese fighting arts as a whole have changed immeasurably. Because of the peculiar way that Japanese combative systems were structured, this innovation often meant that instead of radical modifications within existing ryu, new ryu were created to accommodate new principles or to meet new conditions.

Even within ryu, however, successive teachers often reconsidered, reworked, or added new material. For example, the splendid Maniwa Nen-ryu, one of the oldest historically substantiated schools in Japan, includes *yadomejutsu* (arrow blocking) as part of its curriculum. This practice was probably added in the late 1700s by seventeenth generation headmaster, Higuchi Sadakore. One Nen-ryu practitioner speculated to me that it was added both as a link to a distant historical past where fighters were described in battle-tales cutting or blocking arrows with their weapons, and also as a psychological training for present day students.

Many close-combat grappling systems have older *kata* for use on the battlefield. These go by such names as *kogusoku* or *torite*. In systems such as Kiraku-ryu, there are added sets, often called jujutsu, which are more self-defense tactics for fights in a civilian context.

Higo Koryu, a very old school of *naginata*, explicitly notes a set of forms in their curriculum that was added many generations after the founding of the school (the name "Koryu," was probably applied after its initial development when other newer systems appeared in the Higo area).

Uchida Ryohei, an adept of Shinto Muso-ryu and infamous leader of the Black Dragon and Dark Ocean societies[2] created a system of *tanjojutsu*, which used Shinto Muso-ryu principles with a walking stick. Uchida-ryu "sutekkijutsu" was added as an associate ryu to Shinto Muso-ryu in the Meiji period (1868–1912), when street-fights among political factions frequently involved combat with both solid walking sticks and sword canes.

Also in the Meiji period, the Isezaki Araki-ryu added a group of throwing techniques called *myote* ("marvelous hands") that are surely a response to early Kodokan judo. I could cite any number of further examples, but suffice it to say that *back in the days when koryu wasn't "koryu," successive generations did change the curriculum to suit the times.*[3]

Does Koryu Have Anything New to Offer?

But these arts *are* koryu now. They are archaic martial traditions, using weapons and combat parameters created for battlefields or societies far removed from that of modern Japan, not to mention that of Western countries. That there is considerable information that is definitely applicable to modern conflict (Japanese bayonet methods, started with a base of French bayonet fighting, then augmented with principles and techniques from Hozoin-ryu spear and Toda-ryu short sword, are only one example) does not change the fact that the total "frame" of the arts is largely a consideration of skills needed in a distant past. This essay will, in its meandering way, attempt to track one central question: is there any possibility of innovation within koryu in modern times? I will focus on both the reconstruction[4] of old forms abandoned and the possibility of something new created. I will also discuss who is "empowered" to do such renovation or innovation, and under what conditions this will damage a ryu, or if there are any circumstances in which the ryu will benefit.

Proof of the Utility of Change or Were the Ryu Primarily Warfare Arts Anyway?

Not only do we need to consider the possibility that the ryu are not pristine systems unchanged from their inception, we also need to widen our viewpoint of the old martial traditions beyond a simple interpretation of the word bugei as "warfare arts." It is true that many ryu were once, in part, methods of preparing men (and perhaps a few women) to fight on a battlefield. But if that were all they were, they would not exist today.

In the Sengoku period (1467–1568), we can envision the ryu using the following analogy. Imagine the Rangers not as an arm of the U.S. Army, but as a fraternity-like organization that trained in their own methods, without being totally under Army command. They would be available to the army and on some bases would become the "official" training group for small squad military actions (in Japanese terms, this would be called an *otome ryu*), but in others, they'd have a clubhouse and training camp entirely off base. Leadership would be passed down in some kind of lineal transmission, independent of changes in Army command structure. Strained metaphor, true, but still close to the mark. In a society in which almost every aspect of life was controlled, the ryu, to some small degree, functioned as independent entities. Minimal independence, to be sure, but it was there. This nominal independence of the ryu took on a life of its own, because it continued long after there was any need for the military skills that the ryu taught.

Because some of the early ryu are so enthralling, I have often heard people question why other ryu developed at all. For example, with no disrespect intended, the simple appearing Kurama-ryu or Kogen Itto-ryu, focusing on sword against sword, with straight posture and much simpler, briefer forms, are not nearly as fascinating as some of the schools Westerners so idolize — Katori Shinto-ryu, Yagyu Shinkage-ryu, etc. But one should take a closer look, both technically and historically. Many of the ryu that developed in the mid-to-late Edo period (1800–1868) use quite sophisticated techniques, including wrist attacks, subtle cutting and deflection in one move, and very upright postures that allow much quicker movement on flat ground or the boards of a dojo floor. These schools are far more useful for the period in which they were born than older traditions. This is because they are dueling systems rather than battlefield systems.

To reiterate, *many of the remaining koryu are not warfare arts — they are one-on-one, face-to-face, dueling methods, for use against unarmored enemies.* Although merely screen choreography, the movie *Rob Roy* beautifully portrays this difference. The claymore was a magnificent weapon, which at one point was preeminent on the battlefields of Scotland. Rob Roy, the hero, armed with such a weapon, is forced into a match with a professional duelist from England. Within that context, on a flat wooden floor, in regulated one-on-one combat, Rob Roy is outclassed by the fop with the dueling saber, while in a melee with armored warriors scrambling among the fens and rocks, the situation would almost surely have been reversed.

Within the Japanese systems, the technical differences between battlefield and dueling systems are not so stark, because, whatever the ryu, the weapons and their morphology remained the same. Nonetheless, the continued development of new sword schools cannot only be attributed to a decadent loss of virility. The geniuses of later periods continued their study of the sword so that it was most useful within the environment in which it would be used.

Finally, let us consider the Meiji period. Warriors from a variety of feudal domains banded together to either fight for the shogun or the emperor. They practiced different martial ryu. This could have caused enormous intragroup dissension. Imagine the prickly rivalry of these supremely egotistical men, as one asserted the supremacy of Jikishin-kage-ryu and the other claimed the superiority of Ten-ryu. With only kata practice and no way to "cross-train" among the various ryu, there would have been frequent fights, numerous injuries, and even deaths. If not testing each other with blades, they would have had to do so with heavy oaken weapons. The fighting groups would have decimated themselves from within. However, they had *gekken* ("rough sword" — early kendo using body armor and split bamboo swords). Through this method, men of different ryu could train vigorously together, establish a pecking order, measure each other's skill, and know what to expect from each other in the heat of battle. In a paradoxical sense, kendo made an extremely significant contribution to the development and outcome of the Meiji Revolution. The sporting competition did more to bond the warriors in fighting units than fruitless conversations about the purpose of each ryu's kata, punctuated occasionally by drunken brawls to prove which was better.

Change Can be Degeneration

Nonetheless, the Japanese warrior radically changed during the Edo period, and so did his level of skill as a warrior. Because the Edo period was a time of peace, individuals could choose to specialize in one or another weapon, and no longer worry about maintaining their ability to face any weapon that might be carried onto a battlefield. The sword was now paramount, functioning symbolically and also practically. It was both an emblem of rule and the primary weapon of self-defense for the warrior class. Walking around town with a spear or naginata would have been unusual, somewhat the equivalent of doing so today with a rifle. Spears and muskets were stored in castles for use when necessary. In fact, battlefield skills had so degenerated that, by the mid-Edo period, samurai were often routed in peasant-revolts by farmers using hoes and picks. The samurai would retreat to their castle, arm themselves with muskets and then return to decimate the farmers from a safe distance.

This weakening of the warrior's prowess has mostly continued up through modern times, with a brief renaissance of bugei in the Meiji period, before the traditional ryu were crushed as a source of military power by conscripts armed and trained in Western military methods. This degeneration included a superseding of military tactics, and a concurrent, though not necessarily related, deterioration of martial prowess, accompanied by a weakening of the bonds among the group members and a loss of the obdurate loyalty and trust of the students to his or her teacher.

Sadly, in this day and age, a lot of the ryu have further degenerated into hobbies. Even in Japan, people — with no more fighting spirit nor integrity than any suburban bourgeois — swing practice weapons once or twice a week and are given teaching certificates to pass pale shadows on to a next generation. Although certified by one entitled to issue rank, the participants often maintain a ryu that is as bloodless as a corpse.

One has to remember that nothing focuses the mind like the fear of death. As practitioners' lives are further and further away from the necessity of combat, their intention in practicing changes too. In many of the more modern arts, this is a positive development. The entire development of iaido is a manifestation of this — the realization that there are a myriad of benefits that can accrue in practicing the minutiae of drawing and resheathing a sword, and that some of these benefits accrue when no longer focusing on training for survival in what is now an "as if" fantasy. But in arts that focus on combative prowess, this is a terrible loss. The bulk of jujutsu schools have surely lost their edge, in part because the techniques, when practiced with energy and intention, hurt. Most people today would prefer to avoid pain, and see no benefit in honing combat skills with such dedication that they might be injured in the process. In addition, virile practitioners in Japan (and even other countries, in the few locations where an opportunity to study exists) are no longer drawn in numbers to koryu grappling systems — instead, they go to judo, sambo, K-1, Pancrase, Brazilian jujitsu, and other rough-and-tumble systems, which seem far more aligned with the needs of young men in modern society than systems that teach how to fight with and against small weapons while rolling on rough ground. In the same manner, most people interested in sword arts practice kendo, often with incredible intensity and verve, while many who practice older sword-fighting methods merely go through the motions in rote clashes of wooden practice weapons. That the air sometimes crackles like blue fire in a kendo match while many koryu demonstrations merely circulate that same air in stagnant eddies is regrettable — sports have achieved more intensity and passion than what should be training for facing that cruel line between life and death.

Systems also stagnate by isolation. I recently read an article in a Japanese magazine about Mikami Araki-ryu (also called Sanshin Araki-ryu). What remains of this system is a compendium of mostly impractical grappling techniques. Its sword methods, for which it was once well known, are completely lost. The school has been isolated in a single mountain village, with no new input and no testing of its techniques in well over one hundred years. It is like a fragile hothouse flower, unlikely to survive outside its very specific environment. However, one would also be making a mistake to consider it as a pure, unaltered window in time. Mikami Araki-ryu was once a vital and quite strong system — this is evidenced by its presence in a number of different geographical locations. Its present version most likely bears the same resemblance to that ryu of several hundred years past as a dilapidated, worm-eaten harpsichord, with broken keys and tangled strings, bears to the polished instrument that played so brightly under Bach or Scarlatti's hands.

Creeping rot also occurs through technical contamination. There are two main sources. The most common is when individuals who practice a modern system such as kendo, judo, aikido or *atarashii naginata* use the logic and physical organization of those methods within a koryu they are studying. This is commonplace, and gets even worse each time a koryu makes a devil's bargain with a large modern association such as the All-Japan Kendo or Iaido Federation, erroneously believing that such association with the mainstream will help them survive. What actually happens is that the old ryu are practiced by a few people as a "supplement" to their training in modern arts or perhaps the ryu is trotted out in a "half-time" demonstration at a sports budo get-together.

A second kind of contamination occurs when an individual has practiced more than one koryu, and begins to apply the logic and technique of one system to the other. This is understandable — the person has gotten some confidence in their skill and knowledge in one system and seeing what they believe to be similarities and deficiencies based on that logic/ideology, either unconsciously or deliberately "improves" the second system. As the people who do the latter tend to be arrogantly brash (not necessarily a bad trait for a young warrior!), the instructor must be willing to bring them in check, if they continue to insist on letting their ego drive their learning. Sometimes this needs to be done

KEIKO SHOKON

physically if the student's "improvement" is, in fact, weak; on other occasions, the "improvement" may "work," but it damages the fabric of the ryu itself. It may not fit the parameters of combat for which the ryu was developed. Worse, the inclusion of the alien material disrupts the neuro-physiological training necessary to make the ryu live within one rather than simply exist as acquired information. The student's insistence on his or her rectitude in this instance is a mark of mistrust and disrespect to the teacher.

The flaw here is more with the teacher than the student, because if the teacher cannot require the student to put the ryu, as embodied by the teacher, above their own ideas, group solidarity and eventually the ryu will be destroyed. The "improvements" that such people offer are usually superficial and reflect a lack of understanding — with divided loyalties, they usually have not spent a fraction of the time necessary to really learn the essence of the ryu they implicitly criticize by "fixing" it. Sadly, many instructors in this day-and-age do not have the moral courage to bring this to a halt — and the result is a new generation that practices *champon* ("chop-suey") ryu — a mixture of techniques that has lost what previously made the system unique and powerful.

If the hot-blooded student can temper his or her ideas and contain the energy through embodying a quality called *nyunanshin* ("pliability," but in this case a willingness to be profoundly and pervasively influenced by the teacher), they will emerge as the finest of practitioners. However, if they cannot, then, one way or another, they should leave the ryu, because they are putting forth their own will and ideas as primary.

What is Training in a Ryu Supposed to Accomplish?

The ryu are far more than catalogs of techniques. A living ryu is an incredibly sophisticated method of psychological and physiological training. Through a combination of obsessive repetition of actions while under both physical and emotional stress coupled with the judicious teaching of esoterica that are geared to have very powerful effects on the psyche of the trainee, one literally becomes a living manifestation of the ryu itself. In a very real sense, one embodies the psyche of the founders of the ryu. Without this kind of attainment, marked by a license such as a *menkyo kaiden*, any independent innovation will be destructive of things the person can't even imagine.[5] For example, an il-legitimately "innovative" individual might eliminate a move in a kata because they imagine it puts them off balance, not realizing that it is *supposed* to put the person off balance in a form that is a training in re-covery of balance, or that a form is really a precursor, designed solely to produce some level of somatic organization and reflexes to carry out the "real" combative method, which will be taught later.

To give an example of the idea that the ryu becomes larger than the sequence of the kata, my senior student, in a recent demonstration, completely forgot the third kata in a *chigiriki* (chain-and-staff) set. I de-flected and dodged his attack that came from an entirely different angle than I expected. Not knowing what to do next, he continued to attack me wherever he saw an opening, and we continued in pure improvisa-tion. At the same time, I had to subtly indicate to him an opening so that he could execute a finishing blow with the proper timing and spac-ing that tied the "kata" together rather than annihilate me through the deliberate weakness I had left in my defenses. The techniques were well done, and a rather dramatic, but otherwise unremarkable kata was per-formed/created. I would defy any outside observer to have known which of the four kata, three done by the book, and one by the seat of the pants, was the "new" one. This is an exemplar, which I personally have reached all too infrequently, of what all of us try to accomplish in koryu training. We do not become "masters of form"; instead, we hopefully train long and hard enough that the form "masters" us.

A TAXONOMY OF FOUR KINDS OF RYU — THINGS THAT CHANGE
YET STAY THE SAME

Martial ryu can be divided into several categories. Gunnery and ar-chery schools, close-quarter combat systems, auxiliary systems (every-thing from swimming in armor to signaling with war fans), and military science. The latter, ryu that were most directly concerned with military tactics, were the systems of *heiho* or *gungaku*. It is significant that there is no sentimental or "spiritual" attachment to these systems whatsoever. Those that remained in the Edo period were utterly abandoned in the Meiji, supplanted by the latest equipment and tactics from far superior European methods. No one in Japan, other than a few historians, studies these outmoded tactical systems. It is therefore remarkable that the other three types have been maintained for so long. There is something in them beyond the mere methodology of sword-fighting, horseback-riding, swimming, etc.

Even considering these continued systems, however, the statement that bugei were transmitted unchanged is both true and decidedly not true. *Suieijutsu* (training in swimming for warriors in armor) is, nowadays, practiced in swimming pools more often than rivers. Among other reasons, the "swimmable" rivers in Japan are mostly polluted ditches. *Bajutsu* is another example. The horses used in bajutsu are no longer the sturdy little horses similar to those ridden by the Mongols — they are, instead, the same sleek and graceful riding horses used in modern dressage. The exponent of bajutsu is obviously not training for mounted warfare any more than the exponent of suieijutsu has plans for silently swimming across a river in *oyoroi* (full armor) to take the enemy camp next to the mobile home parking lot.

GRAPPLING WITH THE MYTHS OF CLOSE-COMBAT SYSTEMS

A number of myths have been passed down regarding close-combat systems, the area of most people's interest. We often get so wrapped up in the particulars of various martial ryu that we forget, from a broader perspective, that they were not really that different from each other.

Consider that in the Sengoku period, exponents of dozens of ryu could march in the same armies and fight side by side without tripping over each other. In the technical sense, one might liken the various ryu to modern competing systems in shooting. There are debates about stance, about aim, and other minutiae, but even with the arguments, all such shooters could go through basic training and function in the same squad as soldiers.

It should also be understood that the ryu often served two conflicting aims: the development of military men, who, by definition, function in a group, and also the desire by each of these men to hone individual skills so that they could excel on the battlefield. But even in the Sengoku period, the different ryu were not so far apart that their differences affected military strategy.

Another myth is the idea that fighting was primarily done by members of the *bushi* (warrior caste). This may have been true during the Heian (794–1185) and even the Kamakura periods (1185–1333). But in the Sengoku period, when the martial ryu system developed, the majority of fighters were draftees of a sort: *ashigaru*, peasants or impoverished men, who were samurai in name only. They did not go through many years of formalized training in a martial ryu. Instead, they got the equivalent of basic training — handed a spear, or in an earlier time, a poorly forged naginata (glaive) or sword (referred to as *tsukai sute*, "use-and-throw-away"), a brief period of instruction in cut-and-thrust and maintaining a formation, and off to war they went. They learned on the job. They were led by bushi who, in some ways, could be regarded as an officer class. This leadership role functioned in two parts — some were literally officers, giving orders, and others, trained fighters, led through the example of their valor and skill.

A third myth is that the sword was the paramount weapon of the Japanese fighting man. At least on the battlefield, this cannot be regarded as true. This myth only "flies" due to the cult of the sword passed down within ryu, and, particularly in the West, the false idea that the Japanese never learned group tactics and insisted on fighting in "one-on-one duels en masse" throughout their history. The samurai were originally mounted archers — the earliest term for martial arts is *kyuba no michi* (the way of the horse and bow). Certainly in this period, the *tachi,* used from horseback, was a central weapon, but this changed once warfare changed. With the increased size of armies, the foot soldier became paramount, and close combat developed — first with the use of longer, heavier weapons such as naginata, *nagamaki* (massive glaive), and *nodachi* (massive long sword), which would be effective against both armored foe and rider on horseback, and soon after, by the *yari* (spear). There is no doubt that brilliant swordsmen using smaller and lighter weapons (*uchigatana*) developed methods of defeating those with heavier and therefore slower weapons. But by-and-large, the sword was a "sidearm." Military tactics far superseded brilliance in man-to-man combat with a sword. The preeminent weapons of the Sengoku period battlefield were the spear and projectile weapons. Ten spearmen could occupy the same space as two or three men with naginata or sword. Like the Swiss pikemen, the spearmen dominated the battlefield, until supplanted by the musket. It is quite significant that in the late sixteenth-century invasion of Korea, generals writing back to Japan for more supplies invariably pleaded for more muskets and more spears — not more swords.

What is paradoxical, then, is that the martial ryu, which (generally speaking) emphasize the sword, first developed in a period in which the sword was definitely not the central weapon of war. The response to this statement is predictable: "But these ryu were *sogo bujutsu* (comprehensive arts)!" I will readily grant that ryu were developed and passed down, in part, to maintain battlefield readiness. Schools such as Takenouchi-ryu and Yagyu Shingan-ryu, which taught grappling and close combat with armor and weaponry, were surely of this ilk. So, to a degree, were such schools as Kashima Shinto-ryu, or Tatsumi-ryu, which practiced an array of weapons. But nonetheless, the center of almost all ryu was the sword. Otake Risuke, for example, defined Katori Shinto-ryu to me as a kenjutsu school and stated that much of their work with other weapons was to prepare the swordsman to face them.

Otake is one man, however, representing only one ryu. Let us therefore, take an overview. The *uke* ("receiver" — in the teaching position) used a sword in most ryu most of the time, no matter what the other weapon in the kata. It may then be argued that the sword gave the teacher an opportunity to teach the principals of combat, no matter what the weapon. It may also be suggested that the sword, as the emblem of the bushi, belonged in the teaching position to exemplify the senior's authority.

Nonetheless, it's remarkable how few ryu practice naginata against yari, *kusarigama* against bo, etc. What this indicates is that the ryu served a second primary purpose — politics. The focus on the sword, the weapon of the bushi, in ryu that were primarily the bailiwick of bushi indicates that the ryu were, in part, a training in how to embody the virtues that allowed one to lead and to rule. I believe that the sword, to some degree, served a symbolic purpose. Yes, it could be used for war and was used on the battlefield, but its larger value was in the creation and maintenance of the bushi themselves as a ruling class.

CHANGE CAN ALSO BE RENOVATION

Today, there are no bushi, and in Japan, there are no wars or even duels fought with the cold frost of forged steel. Despite a rather small revival in Japan, led by researchers who form study societies to compare and contrast schools, koryu are dying out. Not all at once, but in small increments. Areas of the ryu are abandoned, being uninteresting to either the teacher or the collective students. Teachers die without passing on the entire curriculum, or, like an isolated population of condors or cranes, there are not enough rare birds left in some ryu to create a new generation of any vitality.

But there are people who have not given up, who, even knowing the ryu are dying, swim directly against the tide of modernization. Paradoxically, it may be the ryu that are willing to revive, reconstruct, or even revise their curriculum that may be vital enough to survive. There is something far different in outsiders, no matter how skilled in their own martial practice, finding a picture book and attempting to imagine their way to a recreation, and real practitioners trying to bring something back to life, as if massaging the blood back into a frostbitten limb. It is this latter I will discuss in my next section.[6]

There is surely a difference of opinion on the validity of renovation in any form. Otake Risuke voiced the conservative view to me several decades ago when he stated that there were sections of his own ryu that had been lost, but that even if he had a meticulous description of how to do the kata, he would not reconstruct them. He stated that written descriptions were insufficient when not accompanied by the lost *kuden* (oral teachings). Without instruction from a teacher who knew the techniques from the inside out, they would have no validity. Otake stated that such reconstruction was useless and had no meaning, as far as he was concerned, and he expressed amused derision when describing another ryu that had consulted with him in their reconstruction of

KEIKO SHOKON

previously abandoned iaijutsu. On the other hand, some instructors equal in stature to Otake believe that if one has an understanding of the essential nature and technical criteria which imbues the entire ryu, one can take an abandoned set of forms and revivify them, based on one's understanding of the rest of the ryu.

Part of this debate is ideological. I believe that Otake's viewpoint is driven by the belief that the school he practices is *tenshin sho* — "bequeathed by divine influence." Divine influence is transmitted through the agency of those imbued with the same *kami* (deity or power). Without such direct transmission, there is nothing of value left to transmit in merely learning some abandoned forms. The other viewpoint is driven by several criteria — that if one can recover even a scintilla of what one's predecessors left, one is paying them and the ryu great respect, much as one does in restoring a house or a painting. In addition, one is also "stating" that to attempt to approach the attainments of the past, one has to work through as much of their legacy as possible. Finally, there is the stance that one is still practicing a fighting system despite its antiquity. If there is untapped knowledge within the system, then one becomes stronger through its study, even if one does not have the benefit of all the knowledge that once existed. The reconstructionist wing expresses a faith in the nature of what *has* been handed down — that it is more than teaching of specific kata, but actually teaches general principles that can be applied elsewhere.

THE TODA-HA BUKO-RYU

When I entered the Toda-ha Buko-ryu in 1977, there were thirty-six forms listed in the compendium of techniques. For the curious, they included five naginata vs. sword, eleven naginata vs. naginata, five naginata vs. spear, five naginata vs. kusarigama, five *kagitsuki naginata* (cross-bar naginata) vs. sword, and five kagitsuki naginata vs. spear. However, fewer than one hundred years ago, there was far more to the ryu. All the kata previously listed were in the *shoden* and *chuden* (beginning and middle) levels. Within that same level, there were also ten bo against sword, and five more kagitsuki naginata against sword. There were higher levels as well: a *dai shihan menkyo* with a number of forms most of which apparently opposed sword in the *ukedachi* role against a number of weapons. This compendium included five naginata forms, five sword forms, five kusarigama forms, five *kodachi* forms, and five *iai aikuchi* forms (quick drawing with a dagger). Finally there was a menkyo kaiden set which had five nagamaki against sword. This array of lost technique and weaponry was a tantalizing fantasy for a number of years. The loss of the kusarigama forms was felt with particular keenness as Murakami Hideo, the headmistress two generations before Nitta Suzuo,[7] was known for her brilliance with this weapon. In the Meiji era, she participated in public challenge matches, took on all comers with naginata or kusarigama, and never lost.

In the early 1980s, Nitta Sensei received a letter from Sakai Shiota Sensei of the Kogen Itto-ryu. The Sakai family had previously provided the copies of the scrolls with the complete compendium of Buko-ryu techniques. Although the family had abandoned their practice perhaps one hundred years ago, Toda-ha Buko-ryu had been passed down in their family for several generations. Suneya Ryosuke, the thirteenth-generation headmaster was also an instructor of Kogen Itto-ryu, and had taught both ryu to the Sakai family. Enclosed with the letter was a sheet of paper with five kata, titled "Toda-ha Buko-ryu naginatajutsu." The names of the kata were unfamiliar, and so were the descriptions of the kata. Nitta Sensei requested that her two senior students at the time, Kini Collins and myself, study these forms and see what we could come up with, simply as a matter of curiosity. The names of all the techniques within each kata and the stances were familiar. Only the order of the movements and the way they were linked were different. Within a relatively short period of time, we returned and presented the results of our study to her. She made some suggestions (the reader should understand that suggestions always are a velvet-toned order) on things we should change to create more of a "Buko-ryu feel." When this was established, we began including these forms within our practice and on one occasion, presented them at Shimogawa Jinja in Kyoto at a large demonstration. What made this especially interesting as a "test" was that Nitta Sensei became ill the day before the demonstration and Ms. Collins and I had to go by ourselves, perhaps the only occasion in koryu history that a prominent ryu was presented in a significant demonstration in Japan with only foreign members representing the ryu. Because of this, we were under rather rigorous scrutiny from the members of other ryu. I remember the focused silence among the spectators as we demonstrated, rather at variance to the more casual glances that other ryu had received. That we were praised to our face counts for little, because Japanese people can be polite in the worst of circumstances. However, gossip is endemic within the koryu world and there was never even a whisper that we, two *gaijin*, had done something that "looked" wrong, even though we had presented kata that no one had ever seen before.

Some years later, I was idly going through the older scrolls and noticed something that should have been obvious before. The names of these five naginata forms, which were not listed in the naginata kata of the ryu, apart from this sheet that looked like it had come from a student's notebook, were almost identical to those of five of the bojutsu kata.[8]

Ms. Collins had already returned to America, and I asked Nitta Sensei if I could have permission to consider the possibility of reworking these back to bojutsu forms. We discussed this in some detail, and Nitta Sensei decided that the forms must have the following general principles: Toda-ha Buko-ryu is a naginata school at its core. For this reason, we had to consider in what way bojutsu would add to the ryu. We noted that there were a number of naginata schools that have staff techniques supposedly intended as practice in what to do if the blade of one's naginata is broken or cut away. Some of these schools, however, are rather naïve, as it would be almost impossible to cut through the shaft near the blade because of the tang, which might extend one to two feet deep.[9] We therefore considered the real possibility of the blade breaking. Each kata therefore has a point in which the "blade" is "broken," and the form continues, in theory, with a jagged piece of metal at the end. This further means that the weapon is not reversed, as it usually is in bojutsu. The theoretical jagged piece of metal and even the *tsuba* become weapons at the end of the shaft.

Thus, its practice was to prepare for a possible but unlikely scenario. The bo, therefore, was to be considered an auxiliary weapon of the ryu, not one of equal importance to the naginata. It should therefore require as little "new" learning as possible. We desired, as much as possible, to maintain the same combat spacing, even though the weapon was one to one-and-one-half feet (30–40 cm) shorter. This was accomplished by changing the grip and placement of the weapon. Rather than bringing the end of the weapon to the hips as we did with the naginata, the strikes ended with the backhand at the chest, providing the same reach to the target (consider an irregular triangle, where both vertices, of unequal length, come to the same peak).

Finally, the intent was to have technique that would be valid with either the ordinary naginata or the kagitsuki naginata (the projecting cross-bar, if present, being another threat to the enemy).

After a period of time, with the help of Meik Skoss and Zama Shoko, the reconstructed kata were presented to Nitta Sensei and she approved them as part of a *betsu mokuroku* (extra compendium). The thirty-six aforementioned kata were now called the *hon mokuroku* (original compendium). The betsu mokuroku was later completed through the reconstruction of nagamaki and kusarigama kata.

The technical descriptions of the nagamaki techniques had been preserved in straightforward unambiguous descriptions, and they were obviously typical techniques of the ryu. The major problem was to establish the morphology of the weapon. It became clear that the type of nagamaki that is really a long sword with a long hilt could not be used with these forms — the sword was far too strong an opponent. Such a nagamaki, at about six-and-one-half feet in length, was too heavy, yet also too short to either cut at the same speed as the sword or crush the swordfighter's defenses from a distance while using Buko-ryu techniques.[10] Instead, a long, massive weapon was totally appropriate. In addition, these kata really did function as a kind of "polishing set." As so-called menkyo kaiden techniques, these "ultimate" techniques must serve as a capstone. They did just that, teaching that above all the marvelous technique one might have previously learned, one has to attack with power and ferocity to make anything work.

KEIKO SHOKON

The reconstruction of the kusarigama forms would take far too long to recount, but one illustrative story is necessary. I eventually presented Nitta Sensei and the ryu with a booklet, with the betsuden forms preserved in drawings, by Zama Shoko, made from photographs of Meik Skoss and myself. Because I was leaving Japan, I was only able to quite hurriedly demonstrate the last reconstructed kusarigama forms to her. Several years later, when she visited me in the United States, Meik and I demonstrated them for her and she was quite pained at what she saw. What I had basically done is taken my modicum of skill in Araki-ryu kusarigamajutsu and made five new Araki-ryu forms against Toda-ha Buko-ryu sword (the ukedachi).

As always, Nitta Sensei's criticism was quite muted — if one is not paying attention, one can simply not notice it. Many Japanese instructors are this way. A failure to realize the gravity of criticism, even that so softly and politely conveyed, denotes an utter failure on the part of the student. Only the puerile and the immature need to be spoon-fed with detailed explanations of "what I meant." Part of training is paying attention to subtleties, because if one can't do it in the dojo with one's teacher, one will have no chance of doing it in combat or other encounters. Being responsive to an instructor's wishes, showing no distress or demurral even when one believes oneself to be "right," is one of the essentials of training. Disputes with one's leader will get one killed in an emergency or cause the death of one's fellows, and therefore, except in the most extreme circumstances, one must learn to suppress one's need to be "heard." In addition, the ryu is an "as if" experience. This is not only in regards to the kata — *one's teacher is always functioning as uke at every moment of contact*. To learn to be that sensitive and aware of another's desires hones the very skills necessary to be equally aware when it counts — when someone means you harm. In fact, one of the primary causes of degeneration of ryu is that students take their instructor's criticism, be it muted or harsh, personally. If the teacher is a man or woman of integrity, it is never personal — except in the sense that the student is given an opportunity to abandon his or her egotistic stance and focus on the needs of the ryu. I am certainly well aware that this is a "system" open to a number of abuses — but it is also the only way that the ryu survived in the past, and the only way they will survive today.

In any event, both Meik and I were quite aware of her dismay. This was particularly my failing as I had been primarily responsible for this reconstruction, and I had, in essence, contaminated something that she had trusted me to preserve inviolate. That the techniques might have worked was absolutely irrelevant. It was not the order of the techniques within the kata or even the angles of attack or defense that was in question. It was the "feel." There was no "Buko-ryu *rashisa*" (flavor). In response to her disappointment, I worked on the kata for most of a year, referring back to the already established kusarigama kata in the hon mokuroku and the writings of Yazawa Isao, the sixteenth-generation headmaster (complete with one photograph of kusarigama against sword). When I presented this final version, the forms met with Nitta Sensei's approval. In her judgment, they were now Toda-ha Buko-ryu, and she decided to formally include them in the betsuden, where there is no pretense that the forms were passed down inviolate since ancient times. At the end of the betsuden scroll, it states that "what is contained here is derived from old records discovered in another region and studied and revived under the authority of the *soke* by her senior disciples."

The Araki-ryu

I have written elsewhere[11] about the syncretic and innovative nature of the Araki-ryu, in almost all factions throughout its history. This continues today. *Ichi koku, ichi den* (one country, one tradition) was a key phrase in the ryu. One was encouraged to leave the area where one studied, put down roots elsewhere and form an augmented or even new line, based on the exigencies of the conditions in which one lived. Some factions, such as the Annaka feudal domain's Araki-ryu specialized in the sword and ended up melding first with Itto-ryu and then early kendo; others such as Maebashi, Isezaki and Kansai Araki-ryu were comprehensive fighting arts, centered around close combat and grappling. Still others, such as the Sakura Araki-ryu and Kumagaya Araki-ryu, became jujutsu schools, specializing in grappling in the context of a civil society — self-defense rather than hand-to-hand combat. Even today, the two current factions of the Isezaki Araki-ryu, usually considered the most conservative, have both revived and reconstructed a number of abandoned kata.

It then should come as no surprise that the faction of which I am a member has also reconstructed kata in a manner similar to that described in the previous section, whenever there have been records available to do so. The kata were culled in a ruthless process through incessant examination and practice of the forms as described in the ryu's records, and also occasional rather dangerous freestyle practice, either with bamboo weapons and lightly padded chained weapons or with wooden weapons without any protection. Our Araki-ryu did not worry overmuch if the forms were "exactly what they practiced" eighteen generations ago. Instead the focus was on whether they lived up to the basic principles of the school, and used the same system of psychophysical organization.

Araki-ryu is an art of survival, with the aim of destroying one's enemies. Rather than a system of all-out attack, such as the Satsuma domain's Jigen-ryu, it was a system of survival by any means available. The attitude, therefore, is predatory rather than aggressive. The ryu uses a number of weapons, all of which one is expected to master. At its core was a method of battlefield grappling, called *torite-kogusoku*. This is not the same as modern grappling, be it judo, sumo, or wrestling, which focuses on unarmed skills in one-on-one bouts. Instead, the idea was to come to very close combative spacing, even body to body, then to stabilize one's enemy's movement, and finish them off with whatever weapon was at hand, while maintaining awareness of potential attack from other enemies. If no weapons were available, one used the natural weapons of one's own body. Thus, although it is grappling, it was never wrestling, nor was it jujutsu.

Our attempts at reconstruction were based on the essential technical parameters of the system, embodied in the person of my instructor, and vivified by the esoteric teachings that give one access to the intentions of the founding fathers. The primary question was whether the form, as we practiced it, was the most suited to accomplish our goal of preserving our life and annihilating our enemies. This is further circumscribed by the requirement that it still be true to the limits of Japanese combat of the period, and further, to the limits of Araki-ryu. Regarding the latter, one of the many misunderstandings people have around koryu is a concern that the ryu's "limitations" make one less effective as a fighter, if, for example, a dash of Shinto-ryu, and three techniques from Chujo-ryu wouldn't make one's own ryu stronger. In fact, combative effectiveness is as much a product of culling and limitation as it is of breadth of knowledge. Joe Frazier was an incredible boxer — he used his short arms and stocky body to become a devastating infighter. His jab was not remarkable, nor was his ability as an outfighter. He developed a style by cutting away what he didn't need. The strength of a koryu is often defined by how wise the founder and successors were in their paring down — not how many techniques they added.

The question, within our Araki-ryu's historical context, was always, "Is this is the best we have?" Therefore if it were found that one angle of attack, one kind of footwork, or even one sequence of moves was better than another, we would adopt the more effective way. As stated before, this would be a stupid violation were these not the choices of an instructor licensed and qualified to make these changes. Ultimately, then, the final decision of how each form was done was that of my instructor. Interestingly, now that I am maintaining my own dojo, it is spiritually very difficult for me to consider changing any of his decisions, even though he told me that he expected me to be willing to do just that. I have done so, but it has the nuance of rejecting a gift given by one of the most important people in my life — it is never an easy move.

Innovation became a natural development that emerged from reconstruction. We might have practiced a form for years and still be stuck on a movement that seemed suicidal — or at least, we couldn't make it work. It might take years before it was decided that the question wasn't simply that we weren't practicing enough. Another "test" was to break the kata — did a movement commit or limit one to such a degree that one became vulnerable if the person didn't attack in the way we

KEIKO SHOKON

expected? Was this then a problem of the technique itself or the way we were doing it? Grappling was the easiest to study, because here you really can test what works and what doesn't without necessarily putting one's life or limb at risk. One can escape, if possible, or simply tap out. At a certain point, it might be decided to simply change the kata — cut a technique, change or alter one, or even a whole sequence. In its utilitarian attitude, Araki-ryu could not tolerate any less than this.

This open willingness towards innovation would be considered outrageous in many, if not most, ryu. I've personally never had the slightest temptation to "improve" the kata of Buko-ryu nor would I have any concept of how to begin. Buko-ryu has an entirely different "personality" from Araki-ryu. This personality is embodied in the phrase, "Araki-ryu (or Buko-ryu) couldn't tolerate…" The ryu, if it is worth anything, is alive. Innovation has to be far more than a personal, egotistical tinkering with technique. It is something that the ryu itself demands, that *not innovating* would be a violation of the ryu.

There is a final question. Is it, then, conceivable, that one could develop new forms of practice, as, for example, Uchida Ryohei did with the short stick? One has to consider the basic assumption of the ryu. To begin with, modern applications using innovations of archaic weapons are idiotic — such things as a double-edged or reverse-edged katana, applications of naginata against police riot shields, or spear forms to face Indonesian silat or Indian silambam are inanities that one would only imagine as a result of peaceful travel, computer games, and modern videos. It is also hard to imagine a reason to create new sword kata to, for example, counter Maniwa Nen-ryu's *tsubame gaeshi* (swallow counter) that one sees on a Budokan videotape, although it may be useful to create forms for a specific goal of training within the context of the ryu.[12] Finally there are limits to how much one can add that might really be new or worthwhile, given the developments in modern times. For example, adding pistol-craft to the ryu makes far less sense than deciding to separately study already established state-of-the-art methods in schools that have carried out rigorous research in the combative use of guns.

However, there is another aspect, one that is different in detail in each ryu one considers. This is the direct application of principles and techniques of the ryu to modern analogues of what the ryu already specializes in. In the case of Araki-ryu, the core assumption was survival in close combat. There are a number of settings in modern day urban life — most, in fact — where the techniques of grappling and stabbing with an armor-piercing dagger would be anathema. It is not self-defense to do something that would put one in jail for many years. Therefore, it seems totally logical, from the perspective of this system, to try to study Araki-ryu as it is applied to twenty-first-century situations. This does *not* mean abandoning the older forms. This means that evasion on foot on city streets or fighting hand-to-hand, without weapons, is perhaps, a relevant question, and that not only is *bakujo* (tying with rope) worthwhile, but so too is securing someone with a tie-strap or duct tape. We already have a precedent for this type of "modern" applications in the previously mentioned myote. Hand-to-hand combat, however, has advanced light-years beyond the crude throwing and striking techniques of Meiji-era jujutsu. There is nothing that forbids an updating — with the inclusion of the cumulative knowledge of all the current active members of the ryu, referring to judo, Brazilian jujitsu, Mongolian wrestling, sambo, kick-boxing, etc. According to the perspective of Araki-ryu, this would only be flawed if: a) we lied about the antecedents of the techniques; b) we abandoned the survival focus (for example, grappling without consideration about leaving oneself open to strikes, or the sudden appearance of small, hand-held weapons); c) we used this modern study to *replace* the older methods; d) if it didn't work.

I have always tried to recruit individuals who are not only of fine character and integrity, but also hopefully stronger and more knowledgeable than I am in some aspect of combat. This requires that they be mature enough to tolerate the knowledge that they may know more or are more skilled at some aspect of what we are studying, and yet still be able to maintain themselves as my student, a loyal member of the ryu. I have, in a sense, held a man like Kano Jigoro as my ideal, rather than a charismatic teacher like Ueshiba Morihei. To me, the essence of

KEIKO SHOKON

a teacher is to lead as a mentor and to be able to gather the strongest people to work together to make the ryu strong. I have no interest or capacity for becoming a spiritual master with uncanny powers, who therefore, has nothing to learn from others, including my students. Yet, ultimately, only I will decide what fits in the body of "my" Araki-ryu, because, as yet, only I am close to its heart.

It is my hope that myote can continue to be a container for the creative and innovative power of future generations. I have no doubt that the central compendium of the ryu, the "koryu" so to speak, will be strong enough that in future generations, it will continue to stand on its own merits. I find practice of these techniques so profoundly rich that I still find myself surprised at how much knowledge each kata contains, like a holographic image of a box from the fourth dimension. No matter which way one moves, it continues to unfold in new ways in three-dimensional space.

Without the "safety-valve" of the myote, it will be quite easy for a "practically-minded" successor, particularly a young one, to say, "Well, the nagamaki and the chigiriki, etc., are useless for the street/police work/military applications/"no-holds' barred" competition, etc. Let's focus on changing the ryu for modern times." The old would be lost, and it would be my guarantee that in a single generation, the essential character of Araki-ryu, its heart and soul, would be lost. More likely still, what remained would be enfolded in some modern system of close-quarter combat, leaving nothing behind but a name. The esoteric teachings are encoded in the handed-down material, and require the "archaic" weaponry to be evoked. Contrary to what some might imagine from my descriptions of this process, any alteration of any of the kata was a painstaking task that required years of study. I have desired to be an embodiment of living history, connected in a chain of lineage now nineteen generations long. It honors my predecessors to maintain a method of achieving victory in the worst of circumstances by honing the kata like one hones a blade. Anyone who knows anything about sharpening a sword knows that it is an exquisitely painstaking and delicate process.

THE QUESTION OF CREATION — "NEO-KORYU"

About eight years ago, I was asked by an individual to teach him "martial arts." He had previously studied aikido with me, but I was no longer teaching that art. For various reasons, I wasn't inclined to invite him into either the Araki-ryu or the Toda-ha Buko-ryu, so I offered him a proposal. I had been interested in Miyamoto Musashi's *Go Rin no Sho* for many years, and so I told him that if he could get together a group of interested individuals, I would be willing to form a "Musashi study group." We'd take a couple of translations (my Japanese certainly not up to the task) and parse out all of Musashi's descriptions of sword technique, *using them, by the way, with a single sword, held with two hands*, as Musashi apparently describes. We had eight members, and practiced for about two years, concentrating on *suburi*, and some simple kata that I devised from my interpretation of Musashi's words in translation. What we ended up with was actually pretty good stuff, which, I believe could certainly endow a sincere student with some significant skills with a Japanese sword. After about two years, however, with the excitement of figuring things out over, I was practicing three different schools, and the difference between the two genuine koryu and my "neo-classical system" was palpable. The power of the two traditions in comparison to my new system was not just a matter of a lineage. The techniques had a substance, a weight, a "juiciness" to them that was lacking from my creation. Each technique evoked a myriad of possibilities. My "kata" only offered one or two variations.

There were hundreds of years of history in the old schools, thousands of men and women gripping their weapons: sweating, bleeding, finding the perfect line, or failing, time and again. There was the weight of rage, fear, grace under fire, blood, death and scarred flesh from the two ryu's earliest days, and the movements hummed and vibrated with all of this. The sword of the "Musashi study group" was possibly somewhat skillful, but all it had was the rather negligible weight of my knowledge. Without a lineage and history, no greater wisdom or strength flowed through my arms.

It was superficial and ultimately boring. So I offered the men, all of sterling character, a choice of entering either the Araki-ryu or the

Toda-ha Buko-ryu, because I was folding the group. Four decided they had gone as far as they wanted with me, and four others decided to join Buko-ryu. Three remain with me to this day.

I therefore believe, both from personal experience and also in observation both in Japan and abroad, that such "homegrown" systems are often uninteresting at best or worse, inane. Some of these are cobbled-together systems from a variety of elements or even ryu, and some, like mine, are made up. They have lost or never had the cultural context, the oral teachings, the spiritual numinousity (kami in Japanese) and lineage, which contains all that make an authentic Japanese martial tradition.[13]

I have no bone to pick with the people who choose to make their own pseudo-archaic system, but it is the equivalent, to me, of listening to a few classical CDs, taking a couple of years of music lessons and deciding to reinvent the symphonic form. I've heard a few "New Age" musicians, who believe they've tapped into a universal source of music, playing improvised concerts of their discoveries. It sometimes sounds pretty, but it's basically noodling on the keyboard.

I'm sure that what such people practice or teach can have great social utility for some or even all of its members, and I don't believe, therefore, that such a system is anathema and "must be stopped." In fact, I believe that most of the practitioners of such systems whom I have met are fine individuals who have benefited from their training. On the other hand, if the creators lie about their origins, they are enacting an obscenity, because dishonesty then permeates everything they do. When they are called on the lies, their students feel it incumbent upon themselves to defend their teacher, a person for whom they offer faith and loyalty. The teacher thereby damages the students' lives in much the same manner as when children try to defend their mother when being teased that she is having an affair with the milkman.

If the teacher is honest about what he or she has created and how the methods are derived, then there is certainly nothing wrong on a moral level. However, one thing still comes to mind. Like most Americans, I was brought up believing that all cowboys were Caucasian. Of course, this was a historical lie — there were many Black and Indian cowboys as well. I learned this looking at a book that described a famous rodeo, with one each of the aforementioned races shown as the top three riders. There were photographs in the book, and despite my previous prejudiced ignorance, there was no doubt that each man was a cowboy. The way they wore their clothes, held their bodies, and their "atmosphere" was identical. Their skin color and personal history was irrelevant.

On another occasion, I saw a photograph of a rather prominent Japanese instructor[14] of a somewhat controversial system of old/new martial arts. On a trip to America, this instructor was wearing a cowboy outfit, complete with hat and boots, and engaged in a series of action poses with a drawn six-gun. He looked painfully odd. This image, I believe, illustrates a mirror image of the difference between the pseudo-koryu and that which is authentic. Those who love their mostly rootless, but innovative arts should consider this well. If they choose to adopt Japanese trappings, then it behooves them to study Japanese culture in such depth that they can express their admiration with some integrity rather than merely playing dress-up.

CONCLUSION

This essay is in many respects an intellectual exercise, because, unless this book is translated into Japanese, I doubt there will be even five readers in this generation who will have the legitimate authority, much less the knowledge of the essential qualities of a ryu, that they might even consider the reconstruction or innovation of anything in the koryu they practice. If one is to treat the ryu, and therefore Japanese heritage, with respect and integrity, it must be understood that reconstruction cannot and should not take place without someone who is the living essence of the ryu overseeing the process. Otherwise, it's simply *samurai gokko* (a phrase that literally means "playing at samurai," with the same nuance as "cowboys and Indians").

The ryu demands that one lives by what the ryu demands. This is inconceivable to most people — perhaps most of my readers here. Frankly, one can only understand this if one becomes nearly insane in the obsessive practice of the ryu; when insomnia is treated not by counting sheep, but by running through the kata, when much of one's available time is spent, in one way or another, practicing the ryu, and as much as is possible, one lives and is ready to die by the principles of the ryu. Any less and it's just a hobby — just physical movement. One becomes so pervasively organized around the activity that one reorganizes on a neurological level to become the activity.

There is no doubt that ryu change. Sadly, most of this change is degeneration — and often unintentional at that. The ryu were once boiling arenas of creative energy, contained within very rigid and very thick walls of tradition. Change used to happen when the pressure of a strong spirit or the requirements of survival demanded it. Now change happens because the techniques may hurt too much, because the weapon is too long for the car or train and is cut shorter, because there is too much to remember and therefore, some sections are abandoned, or because people have other things to do that are more important, be it going to parents' meetings at school, soccer games, or watching a drama on TV. Change happens in koryu. I am quite grateful, in many ways, that it is often so glacially slow. It is sad, however, that there is far more change for the worse than change for the better. It is even sadder that so few people see the ryu as glowing with enough fierce energy that they are considered living entities rather than mere cultural treasures.

What must be understood is that the ryu became something far larger than groups who practiced the best angle to cut on the run. The ryu were created to serve larger ends, and combative practice (and conceivably combat itself) was merely a vehicle towards those larger ends. Few people today anywhere train to acquire the power to act as bushi used to — as movers of a portion of the world. To a custodian of a cultural treasure, all change is potentially poisonous. To a bushi, *appropriate* change was the lifeblood of one's role — to lead, to risk, and to rule.

Renovation and Innovation in Tradition   173

Notes

1   Conch shell, used as signal on the Japanese battlefield.
2   The Black Dragon and Dark Ocean societies were merely the most
    prominent of a myriad of secret societies that promoted a
    charismatic, romantic version of Japanese fascism. Born in the Meiji
    period, many of the original members were unemployed samurai.
    These societies had links to the *yakuza* underworld, among secret
    societies and revolutionary movements in Continental Asia, and
    with the Imperial family. In many ways, these societies exemplify a
    continuation of bushi tradition and morality into modern times.
    Their bloody record of intimidation, riot, political manipulation,
    and assassination belies the superficial fantasies of many Westerners
    regarding bushi morality and behavior.
3   Lest the reader think I do not believe in or approve of the
    maintenance of tradition, nothing could be further from the truth. I
    recently observed two practitioners of Yagyu Shinkage-ryu who
    practice lines that have apparently had no contact for at least two
    hundred and fifty years. There were a few differences that a trained
    eye might pick up, but they were doing the same kata, in an almost
    identical manner. With only a single day's practice, they did these
    forms together with quite remarkable facility. It was thrilling —
    proof of vintage, so to speak, that this ryu had tangible evidence
    that it went that far back with almost no deviations whatsoever.
    Watching was like having a chance to hear Mozart playing his own
    sonatas.
4   This essay will rely on terminology organized by Liam Keeley in a
    work in progress, the first part of which has appeared in *Hop-lite*. I
    am indebted to him for his elegant organization of the terms in
    question.
5   I do not mean that the "menkyo makes the man." If passed on with
    integrity, the license is a tangible symbol of a recognition of the
    level of attainment by a teacher who also has that level of
    attainment.
6   As an intellectual exercise, I once took a book that had verbal
    descriptions of the kata of a ryu I knew nothing about. I followed

the descriptions as best I could, trying to reconstruct the kata from the verbal descriptions. Of course, when I had finished, I simply had five Araki-ryu kata. When I later got a chance to see the ryu in question, the kata bore almost no resemblance at all to what I had fantasized into existence.

7   Nitta Suzuyo took the traditional male name Suzuo when she became soke of Toda-ha Buko-ryu.

8   For many years, we've speculated about how this could have happened. I believe that I recently discovered the answer. The Sakai family faction of the Kogen Itto-ryu has five little-practiced naginata kata. These are the same five kata that Sakai Sensei originally sent to Nitta Sensei. The members of the Kogen Itto-ryu state that these forms were incorporated into the ryu by Suneya Ryosuke. I've seen them on film and it is remarkable how close Ms. Collins and I came, under Nitta Sensei's supervision, to the forms they have preserved. The differences are clearly associated with the different "essence," which includes ways of cutting, spacing, and timing, that typifies the two ryu. It is my personal belief that Suneya wished to include naginata in Kogen Itto-ryu to round out his fighters. However, there would be a number of political ramifications were he to have simply placed five of the traditional kata into the Kogen Itto-ryu. This could have easily enmeshed the two schools in arguments as to who was doing them right. I believe he therefore reworked five of the bo kata using the principles of naginatajutsu that he knew so well. This gave the Kogen Itto-ryu the rounding out he believed they needed without engendering the arguments that were so easy to evoke.

9   Tendo-ryu, I believe, considers the possibility of the entire blade and tang breaking out of the shaft—for this reason, they have jo forms using a staff that was traditionally supposed to reach to mid-forehead—about the length of a shaft with the blade "broken out."

10 The former weapon is not intrinsically ineffective. Hikita Kage-ryu, for example, reportedly has quite strong forms using the long-bladed "sword" type nagamaki. However, the techniques that

the ryu uses are quite different. That the weapon was ineffective in Buko-ryu only meant that it didn't suit Buko-ryu kata.

11 See "Koryu Meets the West" in *Koryu Bujutsu: Classical Warrior Traditions of Japan.*

12 See Amdur, "Koryu Meets the West," for an example of this regarding iaijutsu.

13 I wish to make a clear distinction, by the way, from someone who has studied for a length of time coupled with personal experience, and develops a modern close-quarter combat system integrated within the American, British, or whatever culture of which they are a member. Such a system simply stands or falls on its own merits.

14 I do *not* mean Shimizu Takaji, by the way, in the good-natured photos of his tour of America, looking quietly amused in chaps and boots.

References

Amdur, E. 1997. Koryu Meets the West. In *Koryu Bujutsu: Classical Warrior Traditions of Japan.* Edited by D. Skoss. Berkeley Heights, NJ: Koryu Books.

Keeley, L. 2001. The "Re-Creation" of Traditional Fighting Arts. *Hop-lite: Newsletter of the International Hoplology Society*, no. 11: 4–7.

Nelson, A.N. 1974. *The Modern Reader's Japanese-English Character Dictionary.* Second revised ed. Rutland, Vt. and Tokyo, Japan: Charles E. Tuttle Co.

Lieutenant Colonel George Bristol, USMC, is a career Marine who has risen from the ranks. He has served extensively in infantry, reconnaissance, and special operations billets in areas including Somalia, Bosnia-Herzegovina, Central America, and the Far East. He began training in judo in 1966 and training in Shinkage-ryu heiho in 1995. He is presently in command of the Third Reconnaissance Battalion. He has completed a biography of fellow Marine and longtime idol, the legendary Donn F. Draeger. His perspectives in koryu are always from the perspective of his profession — U.S. Marine — and its mission — combat.

Keiko Shokon

THE PROFESSIONAL PERSPECTIVE
THOUGHTS ON THE KORYU BUJUTSU
FROM A UNITED STATES MARINE

George H. Bristol

I first encountered the *koryu bujutsu* in the pages of Donn F. Draeger's seminal three-volume set, "The Martial Ways of Japan." I was young, eager, and totally convinced that I was on the path of the professional warrior. I can remember vividly thinking that my expertise in judo, boxing, and wrestling gave me incredible advantages in my chosen endeavor, the u.s. Marine Corps. I skimmed rapidly through the first two volumes, *Classical Bujutsu* and *Classical Budo*, and on to the third volume, *Modern Bujutsu and Budo*. I wondered why Draeger — a Marine who, like myself, came from the ranks and became an officer — would hold these classical weapons-based arts in so high a regard. After all, wasn't he a *judoka* of world renown? Wasn't he a weightlifter, hard-core physical trainer of champions, and leatherneck like me? What had set him on this course into a world seemingly without ranking, without fanfare, without spotlight? These questions haunted me for years as I matured both as a Marine and as an exponent of the martial ways. While I remain somewhere along the road in both endeavors, they are inextricably linked in my mind and actions, and, after twenty-six-plus years, I have come to realize that the common ground lies in the training methods, mind-set, and principles of the *koryu*.

I am in the late summer/early autumn of my military career; I am closing in on thirty years of service to country and Corps. I have served in a variety of assignments, both in conventional and special operations. I have been led by heroes and have led some of the finest men and women that this great country produces. I have been an active duty Marine in both peace and conflict. I came to the Corps as a kid from New England, with no preconceived notions other than a boyish yearning for excitement and adventure in places far away. Deployments and travels to the Far East, Middle East, Africa, Central and South America, and Europe have given me a glimpse into other cultures and aspects of life that most of my generation only read about. Adventurous and exciting? Certainly. However, the stark reality of shots fired in anger and the grim facts of conflict do not match the idealistic, John Wayne-style Marine Corps of my youthful dreams. There is no technicolor battlefield or swaggering hero. There is only a mission, uncertainty, and Marines who depend on leadership, combative function, and the teamwork that is fostered by tough training to survive.

Similarly, my martial arts experience has traveled from the more flashy, sport-oriented modern budo — specifically a love of judo and jujutsu — to the austere, battlefield-functional environment of the koryu. Once as a young man, I was told by someone, "Wait until you see guys like Draeger … they are awesome." I remember clearly thinking, "Wait until Draeger sees me…." I think I honestly believed at one point in my life that I could "take" most any opponent. What the term "take" meant to me then and now is radically different. It was not until I had been in combat that I realized that the empty-handed techniques I had learned were largely for sports-based combatives. Not long after those realizations, I began to see where men such as Donn Draeger had been headed, and I began to search anew. The koryu bujutsu — difficult to find, difficult to do — were clearly the path, though the way was obscured by shadows, misconceptions, and pretenders.

Koryu training is different than any other martial discipline I have encountered. The responsibility to the tradition is immense, the focused concentration is palpable, but there is a no frills "get to the point" sensibility that fosters proper learning. In the tradition in which I train, Shinkage-ryu heiho, the very name, *heiho*, indicates this difference. The simplest definition of this term is "the art of war."

Two aspects are characteristic of training sessions — exertion and silence. There is little standing around, but if one pair is working alone, all others are watching, intently. One voice, the teacher's, talks if necessary, and the corrections are succinct. Questions are asked and answered, a few teaching points offered for all, and training resumes.

There is an air of focused application, with no outside distraction of job or family talk to interfere. Working with weapons at close proximity is a serious undertaking.

Supplemental training — combative conditioning of any type — is not mentioned. Rather, it is a given that if you are at the training area, then you are ready and fit enough to train. If you are not fit, you do not last. Injuries are indicated without emotion and dealt with. The teacher knows each student's capabilities and trains each to their fullest capability. A dignified, austere ceremony is conducted at the start and end of each training session; the participants acknowledge the tradition and headmaster.

My own instructor, Hunter Armstrong, has trained and persevered for many years in order to become a koryu teacher. Physically capable and mentally agile to an extreme degree, he is both a commanding and formidable persona. He is exacting in his instruction and his responsibility to Shinkage-ryu heiho. Coming to study with him as a Marine with no shortage of ego myself, I am continually amazed at his energy and professional approach. I am no quick study, and yet, he remains patient and vigilant, correcting my many errors, and giving me as much as I can absorb at my present level. It is particularly rewarding to me that he accepts my combat experiences with the same interest as I accept the *kuden* transmission of combative techniques of the *ryu*.

Throughout my experience in koryu, I have been amazed at how utterly inept I can be in performing the most simple movements. I have struck many of my opponents out of sheer incompetence; often I have been struck for the very same reason. Lastly, I have learned, painfully, that there are engagement factors that I will have to wait years even to see, not to mention attempt. Comfort and confidence in koryu is a relative thing. I rarely have the feeling of smoothness and fluidity that I have encountered in other physical aspects of my life.

I have found a similar lack of fluidity in combat situations. I reflect that I was lucky to "live to tell." I recall uncertainty, confusion, fear, and fatigue. Things that I had thought were long-ago "grooved" muscle memory — weapons magazine changes, cover, and concealment — were out of sync and staccato, rather than smooth and fluid, as they had been in training.

Sports, including many of the modern martial arts, afford a rigidly controlled environment with little variation. Combative endeavors are just the opposite, uncontrolled and offering endless variations. Victory in sports is replaced in combat by survival — a powerful stimulant but also a wild card. I believe that koryu training has more in common with combat training than it does with sports, and for this reason it has been particularly helpful to me as a Marine in combat.

The following thoughts are from the perspective of someone whose chosen profession depends on his ability to internalize timeless principles and put them into action in a completely uncontrolled environment. The life of an arms-carrying professional has been my calling; training in the koryu has aided me in that calling.

TEACHER-SCHOLAR

The martial arts world I came from, the judo world, is highly structured, and the teachers rule above the students. Even the titles, the *yudansha* (the "graded") and the *mudansha* (the "ungraded") echo the distance between the peak of Olympus and the ocean bottom. I was used to the pecking order; I thrived as I prospered, and I became a much tougher examiner than those who had examined me.

Marine Corps' Recruit Training (Boot Camp), at least as I remember it, offered no big surprises; it mirrored the judo environment in many ways. There were drill instructors for *sensei*, all-knowing and distant. There was a "do it, do it, do it" mentality with no questions asked; if you could do it fast and with motivation, you were doing right. Testing was conducted in a highly scheduled curriculum. There was no secret of what was coming: "just do it" as you had been taught and it would be right. My drill instructor's definition of discipline was "instant willing obedience to orders." Ironically, one of my earliest memories of judo was the unforgettable practice of "shrimping." Crawling back and forth for thirty minutes as several brown belts watched, a friend of mine asked, "Why are we doing this?" The reply came back, "Two reasons ... one, because I said so ... two, because I am a brown belt!" Drill instructors would certainly have understood the train of logic.

However, the environment that breeds a professional needs none of that logic. Now in my mid-forties, I consider that time in judo — as well as my experiences in Boot Camp, Officer Candidates School, and The Basic School — as rites of passage on my way to becoming what I term "the trained man." Rites of passage are a part of almost any organization that must conduct a hard mission. I have attended many military schools, most of them very physical in nature, and I believe that a tough physical price is much needed to identify and train those willing and able to endure. I spent a long period in grappling arts along the same vein: wrestle-offs, weight cutting, *randori,* and performing as a throwing dummy for higher rankers. It was not a bad thing, but neither has it been a crowning achievement.

Training and preparing for combat is rigorous. It must be realistic and tough. However, it should also be a professional environment with all goals focusing on a positive end. I would like to emphasize that I said positive — not easy. Once again, koryu has the structure and the function to create this setting. The key lies in both the teacher and the student. Major General John A. Lejeune, one of the Corps' fabled leaders, termed the ideal between senior and junior Marines a "teacher-scholar" relationship. I believe that if this situation can exist in the koryu training environment, then it can — and must — exist in the military combat training environment.

Is a tradition such as Shinkage-ryu heiho far removed from the modern military? Many would say yes. But in the last ten years, I have interviewed many from the Marine Raiders, one of our most decorated combat units from World War II, and I have found parallels that bear mentioning. Most of the Raiders will tell of tough, realistic training that included thirty to fifty mile marches in full combat gear, endless immediate action drills in darkness, and shooting and close-in fighting that was "so real that it was scary." But there are just as many stories of the "hard men with gentle hearts" who were the leaders of the Raiders. The accounts of learning from the trainers and then applying those skills and knowledge in combat are legion, and the accounts are devoid of bragging, self-importance, or personal glory. They are all Raider stories told by members of the unit.

The common link is the teacher/leader and the student/scholar. In the koryu, I have never been the most fluid or quickest in my training, but I know that I will be taught to fully develop to my maximum capability. This certainty allows me to fully concentrate on the structure of the training environment. I have little concern for the level of other students — whether they are ahead or behind me in training is irrelevant. My allegiance to the tradition is to do my best with maximum effort and intent. Rankings and grading are between teacher and student; they are never mentioned in training.

I have found a parallel in certain units in the military. While rank is always present, the type of environment described above is optimum for unit efficiency. The hierarchy is established and if mission accomplishments outweigh individual goals, then a smooth flow occurs. Some of my best memories of success in the military are from special operations in which a relatively small band, a "company of like-minded men," pushed for a common goal. Billet assignments, individual accomplishments, and perks and hardships were secondary. A leader led and all others fell into their respective places, each contributing to the best of their abilities and training. Despite the danger and tenure of the assignment, the bond formed was not unlike a koryu tradition — a tradition of excellence.

The beauty of the koryu is that it fosters such a structure, given the proper teacher and student. The Greeks have a saying: "The Gods from above smile warmly on a gentle teacher." I do not think that gentle means easy; rather, it means one who can train each to his fullest. There is a story of a koryu teacher and one of his young, talented students observing a training session some years ago. One of the exponents had one leg much shorter than the other; his technique was not smooth. The young student remarked, "Sensei, that one will always have trouble." The teacher replied, "No, that is not the way to look at it. He should be developed to the best capability that his particular structure allows for. That is the job of a teacher." The Gods, whoever they are, surely smiled warmly that day. The teacher? Donn Draeger. The younger student? Hunter Armstrong.

BASIC FUNCTION FIRST — REFINEMENT AS TIME PERMITS

One of my first "light bulb moments" in koryu occurred after my training in Shinkage-ryu had barely begun. I was participating in an International Hoplology Society Board of Directors Meeting with Hunter Armstrong, Liam Keeley, and Meik Skoss in Sedona, Arizona. On the first night of our meeting, some video was played while we ate and relaxed. I listened, totally fascinated, as these three longtime koryu exponents dissected and discussed various aspects of the engagements displayed. Despite the old, grainy quality of much of the film, aspects of the weapons, exponents, and *kata* were brought into vivid detail by their commentary. However, I could see few, if any, of the myriad details that were being discussed. That night, I watched the film again, searching for clues, wondering if it would take me twenty or so odd years before I could speak or act with any authority.

One particular engagement drew my undivided attention, for the short clip had brought the three to silence earlier that evening. It showed Donn Draeger, in his fifties, armed with a *kusarigama*, closing in quickly and exploding into action. After he completed the strike, a lone comment — "he was pure intent, wasn't he…" — was spoken. Years later, that evening reverberates still. Simple, violent, and totally focused on the elimination of a threat, Draeger's actions are at the heart of combat.

The koryu bujutsu were designed for the battlefield. The techniques of each tradition were codified to function, for the particular group, in an era where daily fighting was the norm and the harsh reality that lethal engagement would occur in a warrior's lifetime was ever-present. The system of combat with all applicable weapons was designed so that basic function/proficiency could be gained relatively quickly in a two- to three-year period. Basic function, in realistic terms for that era, meant the ability to survive intact. Refinement came during periods of relative peace where training in battlefield-proven technique could be conducted. Those who trained, fought, survived, and refined became the teachers of the tradition. However, basic function was far more important than refinement, given the nature of battlefield engagement and the relative chances for survival.

At the heart of that basic function is intent. Nothing matters more in koryu training than the intent that drives an exponent to close with his opponent. Whether the *naginata* is manipulated smoothly or not, if the cut is made, it is a good cut. In *sojutsu*, the *maki*, disruption of the opponent's weapon, is important. It is not nearly as important as the *tsuki* — the thrust. I am continually amazed when I watch the fluidity of longtime exponents of koryu. But perfection of skill does not take the place of intent — and it never will.

This factor constantly faces the military professional, particularly in a leadership position. A Marine Corps legend, Colonel Anthony "Cold Steel" Walker, told me once that "the standard that exists in your mind as a leader will never be met by your Marines. You will always want them to be more fit, better shooters, more lethal. But you must go with what they are when combat occurs. That reality — and the Marine's blood, sweat, and heart — must carry the day." Leaders from any age have encountered and dealt with this conundrum; troops can never have enough training, and intent is the factor that distinguishes the survivors. It was not uncommon, and World War II bore this out in stark detail, for Pacific theater Marines to be sent into combat with far less than one year of training. Those who survived were sent back to train other groups preparing for combat; post-war veterans established the training courses for the future.

If we survive, thanks to the ferocity of our intent, then refinement, as an individual, a group, and a Corps, can and should occur. I often watch that clip of Draeger and, now, the lesson is clearer. The basic function — intent — must be there. All who saw and trained with him knew that. That intent drove the refinement that has an old, grainy eleven-second engagement with a seemingly archaic weapon teaching combative lessons to a new generation of Marines. That film clip is one of the first things that Marine Corps Martial Arts Instructor-Trainers see when I train them. The weapon and the costume do not matter.

The class title is "Combative Intent," and I use the film clip to spur that basic function.

There is No Kata — Only Engagement

The very mission of the koryu bujutsu differs from what I will term the modern martial arts. Donn Draeger described the budo as "the way of individual self-perfection," while the bujutsu are "the way of group self-protection." This dichotomy has clearly formed my own bias, for I am not in the business of perfecting myself for individual gain. A common guideline that covers the scope of what a career military man seeks is this axiom: "eliminate the threat at hand; protect the force; accomplish the mission." Nothing that we do in the military should deviate from mission accomplishment. Koryu has its own mission — the mission of engagement for protection of the tradition, the group, and the individual. The vehicle for mission accomplishment lies in the prearranged movement patterns known as kata.

The prearranged movement patterns of Shinkage-ryu are either simply complex or complexly simple. However, in both cases, the layers that compose them gather tightly to form a lifetime of study. Moving with a weapon — or series of weapons that includes *yari,* naginata, *nagamaki, odachi, tachi,* and *kodachi* — is the first step. Wielding these weapons is not easy in the simplest arena; moving against an opponent similarly armed is harder still.

Kata, at least for me in younger years, were odious. I always scoffed at the idea of something staged or prearranged. But the reality of combative culture has proven clearly to me that the best way to go to the edge of realism is through a prearranged pattern. The infinite possibilities that exist within the pattern are dependent on the training level of the exponents, the terrain of the engagement location, and the combative intent. Surprisingly, the ways to cut with many of the weapons are few; the target areas are limited to the best possible structural damage. But the *maai,* the combative engagement distance, changes with weapon integration and skill level in a dynamic movement cycle.

Once the basic function of the pattern is mastered, the second step — engagement of the opponent to cause systematic destruction —

begins. When using the term "engagement," I offer this explanation: dominate him mentally from approach to close; enter having taken into consideration all available weaponry, terrain, and intent; and systematically take him out so that he will never again rise against you or those you fight with. For the military professional, this step lasts for a lifetime. In my career, I have seen an exponential rise in the use of technology. However, regardless of the weapon or gear at my disposal, I must deal with a threat and accomplish a mission through these steps of engagement. It is never scripted, never the same, never easy. Certain basic principles apply, and those principles rule in all environments. Koryu teaches this intimately.

One of the first patterns learned in Shinkage-ryu, *hassei-ho jodan*, is indicative of this process. The first clash, *gasshi uchi* (mutual strike), reveals the heart of engagement. In order for the exponent to make a cut, he must move in to potentially take a cut. While it is established within a pattern, there are many variables — distance, timing, targeting — and the outcome is anything but certain. The most relevant axiom I can think of in a military sense is the mission statement of the Marine Corps rifle squad: "Locate, close with, and destroy the enemy by fire and maneuver or repel his assault by fire and close combat." However, to locate and close with an opponent means that he is locating and closing with you. A pattern? Yes, in a way. But a pattern of endless sides and angles, all dictated by the actions of the participants. Its end function, the catalyst and driver of all combative endeavor, is to eliminate the threat at hand. Training that embodies this shifting complexity is invaluable to any professional, and I have found that, with proper mind-set, the koryu kata combined with high-end combative conditioning is the martial skill set closest to actual combat that I have encountered.

The many patterns of Shinkage-ryu heiho continue to provide me with a structure that allows for endless study and application. For example, *enpi* — one of the oldest patterns — is conducted with naginata, odachi, and tachi; it can also be executed with dissimilar weapons (naginata vs. odachi, etc.). Within this realm, I have begun to discover that my teacher's oft-repeated phrase, "One Mind, Any Weapon," is particularly germane and has wide-ranging military application.

For example, I have been in threat areas in which Rules of Engagement (ROE) have limited my weaponry. In Somalia, there were threat levels in which the rules regarding the ability to engage were varied. Often, the ability to use force was dictated by political factors and overtones; after all, it was a stated "humanitarian mission." And it was — until the firing started. The same holds true for the Balkans: it was simply not a clear "shoot or be shot" scenario. However, in each case there was a threat, often lethal, a force to be protected, and a mission to accomplish. Regardless of my personal choice of engagement criteria, when the threat was present, I was forced to deal with it. ROE, terrain, or any other factor did not change this. My reaction to the threat, offensive or defensive, told the tale. The function of the "One Mind, Any Weapon" adage was with me over and over again: weapons and terrain can change, but the mind must constantly deal with the threat at hand. There is a pattern, regardless how blurred; the military professional marches on to conflict with some general idea of what he will face. But his "set-piece" battle ends with the first shot. He will deal with whatever comes for himself, and those he enters with, as it comes to him — and be pre-emptive if he can. Reflection on these situations, at least on a personal level, has drawn me closer to the training parameter of the koryu: there is no kata — only the process of engagement.

EASY TO DO JUSTICE — MUCH HARDER TO DO RIGHT

Today's society is one of automation and comfort. Technology exists to make it easier for humanity to function. Comfort is a natural by-product of that same state. There are machines that drive us, write for us, correct our spelling, and keep us in shape. I saw recently a machine that emits a series of electro-impulses designed "for those too busy to work out. Just attach and get a simulated exercise period." The just reward of our vast intellect is that we can sit and view the world from our computer terminal — we have that ability. However, while that justice makes life easy, it does not necessarily mean that it is right.

A lesson of koryu that I find invaluable is that while the weapons and patterns do not change, the exponent does. Consistent, focused training and proper mind-set creates an ethos that is both just and right. This ethos is timeless, nationless, and faceless; it bears only the echoes of a creed, and it is a warrior's creed. The tight control that most longtime exponents maintain over their respective traditions is due in no small measure to the adherence to that self-same creed. Austere, "far from the madding crowd" training is the norm; little fanfare is given save amongst those inside the tradition.

Three aspects of training that I have encountered solidify the concept of what is just and what is right. First, training in koryu is conducted in a natural training environment, outside and on rough ground. Obstacles, footing, terrain, and weather are a factor. Second, repetition of patterns and technique is never perfect, and as a result, no one ever "gets it." Rather, one keeps at "it" for his lifetime. And finally, rather than excuses or opinions, one wins by winning, that is, maximum effort. None of these three are easy, and in reality, most martial arts practitioners are simply not willing to put in the effort. Training in a climate controlled indoor facility offers level ground and sure footing. Competitions, grading, and sub-grading offered by many teachers foster the illusion of "getting it." Many who are marginally qualified teach rather than train. Old, established traditions are splintered, divided and reconstructed for ease of learning and self-aggrandizement.

Sadly, this same lack of effort exists in the military. The tough assignments that offer little reward save service to country are often avoided in favor of the "career track" — a series of assignments benefiting the individual rather than the organization. Technology offers easy alternatives to training — the common term is "simulation." It is far easier to go for a jog than to hike in full combat gear. A creeping doctrine called "operational risk management" has eroded much of the individual initiative once afforded leaders.

The professional can afford neither this blurring of justice nor to stray from what is right. The theme that exists within the fabric of the koryu and the warrior creed is that one trains for certainty: the certainty that conflict will occur. However, one educates for uncertainty

— the time, place, weapon, health, opponent, and a myriad of other factors. But everything that is encountered along that path can be mitigated or litigated with a rationalization.

Some years ago, an anthropologist told me "the human being is the only species that will actively seek discomfort." But today, I often wonder. Recently, my much-respected training partner, Pat Lineberger, joined me for an evening session in Manoa Park in Hawaii. We began as a driving rainstorm blinded us, and, slipping and sliding, we went through Shinkage-ryu heiho. Later that night, I returned to find that a Marine unit had canceled a training evolution due to "inclement weather." Pat Lineberger is in his mid-fifties and had worked a fourteen-hour day to fit the training into his schedule. The Marines' average age was twenty-one.

The next day, I inquired of the unit leader as to why he had canceled. He told me in no uncertain terms that with the weather he deemed it untenable. He said, "Sir, it was my call, and I feel that it was just." Later, I called Pat and asked if he had even considered canceling. He seemed surprised, saying, "Training is training, and weather is not a factor. What's right is right."

I concur with the latter and am sorry for the former, though sadly, I am not surprised. For it is easy to do justice — much harder to do right.

THE CAPABILITY TO KILL — THE COMPASSION NOT TO

In one of the patterns in Shinkage-ryu heiho, the engagement has both exponents at very close quarters, exposed and poised simultaneously. One explanation given to me was that "you are, in effect, playing with the distance, seeing how close is too close, how far is ineffective." Working with a live opponent, despite familiarity with the pattern, makes for a dangerous game. One koryu exponent stated, "It is really not a game — except in the sense of life and death."

To strike and kill is really not a difficult act. Many of the weapons used in koryu are razor-sharp blades, and it merely takes a placement to cut to the bone and cause structural, and often fatal, damage. Similarly, to fire a weapon and kill is simple. Today's arsenal can reach out and touch from astounding ranges with systematic accuracy. Even in the realm of bow hunting, technology makes for little chance of missing. I recently observed a compound bow with a laser sight, stabilizer, and a "let-off" system that allowed for the weakest archer to hold his nocked arrow at full draw for an almost indefinite period.

However, the difference between a warrior and a thug rests in his ability to balance the capability to kill with the compassion not to kill. The only way that balance can be achieved is by proper training and ethics. This mind-set can only be attained by consistent training that is integrated and principle-based. Hunter Armstrong told me once that Shinkage-ryu heiho is "far more than technique. It is the way one lives his life." He has trained for years in Japan under the tutelage of a wise and talented gentleman-warrior, Kato Isao, Kancho Sensei. But the lessons are not limited to those of longtime practice. Recently, I asked his son, also named Hunter, if his friends had seen him train, for he is an outstanding exponent. He replied simply that "he didn't talk about it to them; training is something he did with his Dad and the ryu." Daughter Samaire echoed similar thoughts; training is something that "is a part of me — always."

Recently, a Marine was discharged dishonorably for killing his wife, using a martial arts choke-hold he had learned in the Corps. He lamented that he had "let the Corps down" and offered his regrets. I was struck by his ease in describing how he had accomplished the act and his lack of regret that he had taken a life. His actions were not those of a Marine; they were those of a thug.

After reading about the incident, it occurred to me that I was much closer to the Armstrong children than I would ever be to this now imprisoned murderer. All four of us have the capability to kill, and two of us have had occasion to do so. The difference is in the training. Along with the physical requirements, there is an ethical responsibility to deal with the blossoming lethality gained. For military professionals, these decisions must be made in the "fog of war." But regardless of the uncertainty, the training must encompass the tenuous balance — when and when not it is right to take life. A warrior in any age must function in the society he protects. The term "ethical warrior" has mystical connotations, but it is germane. The taking of life is easy; it is, in effect, a cycle of function, whether from a *junsei* cut with an odachi or the squeeze of a trigger with an M16A2 rifle. Training must be structured in such a manner to deliver the neural drive to close without hesitation. However, it must also give equal measure to the disciplined response to walk away.

BUAI SHINKEN SHOBU

In the "Foreword" to Diane Skoss' initial work, *Koryu Bujutsu: Classical Warrior Traditions of Japan*, I wrote that "conflicts will occur, and warriors will engage. Mind-set — and the training that fosters it — will prevail. And mind-set — the combat mind-set — is the heart of the koryu." I remain true to that statement, as I believe does the koryu.

Having said that, does one need to be in the military to fully appreciate the nature of the koryu? Are only those who are, like their Japanese feudal era antecedents, given the right to bear arms able to unlock its timeless axioms and teachings? Can one who will never have the opportunity to go into harm's way for his country or clan be able to ever truly call himself a warrior?

I believe that the secrets of the koryu are available to those who are not professional warriors. The koryu bujutsu survive not just for those with a military calling. Rather, the koryu can exist for those who seek to stand for something timeless, dwelling in a state of becoming and looking not to a distant future, but rather an eternal present. The preservation of these extant traditions, so far from the bright lights of the modern martial arts world, is a noble calling. The lack of pretense, the austere training environment, and lifelong pursuit toward a highly elusive goal are all prime reasons for continued study.

But for myself, I seek solace in the words written by the late Donn Draeger in *Modern Bujutsu & Budo*, in which he defines the classical bujutsu in the concept of *buai shinken shobu* — "combat to the death between professionally trained and highly skilled equals" (58). Combat changes everything. There is no next time — only the time at hand. I know that my perspective is bound up in that concept, and it is a professional perspective: one that is the way I have chosen to live, both as a Marine and as a man. The Marine Corps is the organization, but the koryu is the path. It is a path that is walked by few, but it has stood well the ravages of time.

I pray that it always will.

References

Draeger, D.F. 1973A. *Classical Bujutsu.* The Martial Arts and Ways of Japan, 1. New York & Tokyo: Weatherhill.

———. 1973B. *Classical Budo.* The Martial Arts and Ways of Japan, 2. New York & Tokyo: Weatherhill.

———. 1974. *Modern Bujutsu & Budo.* The Martial Arts and Ways of Japan, 3. New York & Tokyo: Weatherhill.

Skoss, D., ed. 1997. *Koryu Bujutsu: Classical Warrior Traditions of Japan.* Berkeley Heights, N.J: Koryu Books.

INDEX

A

aikido   48, 152
aikijujutsu (unarmed techniques of *aiki*)
    Daito-ryu   115
aikuchi (small dagger)   160
Aizen Myo-o (Buddhist deity)   45
Aizu *han* (present-day Fukushima
    Prefecture)   112 - 113
Amdur, Ellis   14, 50, 55, 73 - 74,
    81 - 82, 99, 144
Analects, Confucian *(Rongo)*   24, 77
    See also Confucius, Mencius
Araki-ryu   50, 163 - 170
    Annaka *han*   164
    bakujo (tying with rope)   168
    Isezaki Araki-ryu   147, 164 - 165
    Kansai Araki-ryu   164
    Kumagaya Araki-ryu   164
    Maebashi Araki-ryu   164
    Mikami Araki-ryu   151 - 152
    modern applications of   168
    myote (marvelous hands)   147, 168
    - 169
    Sakura Araki-ryu   164
    torite-kogusoku (battlefield
        grappling)   165
aristocrats, Japanese   130
armor
    oyoroi (full armor)   155
    techniques for use when wearing
        91, 97 - 98, 154
    See also *kogusoku*
    tosei gusoku   97
Armstrong, Hunter   181, 185, 192
Asari Matashichiro Yoshinobu
    114, 116
ashigaru (foot soldiers)   97
atarashii naginata   80, 152

B

Bach, Johann Sebastian (1685–1750)   35,
    58, 152
bajutsu (horseback-riding)   155
battlefield systems
    See combat systems
bayonet   147
Beaubien, Ron   13, 86
benefits of training in *koryu*   80
Benkei   66
Black Dragon Society   147
bo (staff)   157, 159, 161 - 162
Bodiford, William M.   14, 128
bogu (protective equipment)   114, 123
bojutsu (staff techniques)   161
bokuto (wooden sword)   98, 124
boxing   179
Bristol, Lt. Col. George H.   15, 178
buai shinken shobu (combat to the death
    between professionally trained
    equals)   193
Buddhism   14, 18, 30 - 31
    Aizen Myo-o (deity)   45
    clergy   130
    kuji (nine characters)   121
    Marishiten (deity)   116
    pedagogical systems   130
    tantra   130
    Zen   18, 24, 31, 117
budo (martial ways)   70, 187
    after World War II   79
    benefits of training in   80
    in the West   36
    modern organizational structures
        56, 152
    modern sport forms 13, 151 - 152,
        165, 182
    self-development in   80

budoka (martial arts practitioner)   36, 66
Budokan
   See Nippon Budokan
bugei (military disciplines)   17, 145, 148
   See also *koryu, koryu bujutsu*
bugeisha (martial arts practitioner)   37, 39 - 40, 42, 48, 60
bujutsu (martial techniques)   187
   See also *koryu bujutsu*
bushi (warriors)   25 - 27, 38, 123, 132, 156 - 158, 173
   ashigaru (foot soldiers)   97, 156
   combat training of 156
   ronin (unemployed former warriors) 132
   samurai   23, 36, 134, 150
   travel restrictions   94

C

calligraphy 77
Carradine, David   25
certification in *koryu*   154, 184
   See also *menkyo*
chajin (tea ceremony practitioner)   55
chambara (samurai movies)   36
Chambers, Quintin   viii, 36
change in *koryu*   14, 42, 44, 52, 95, 145 - 147, 155, 169, 173
chanoyu (tea ceremony) 132
chess (*shogi*)   132, 137
Chiba Chosaku   66
Chiba Shusaku Narimasa   114, 116
Chichibu area (present-day Saitama Prefecture)   115
chigiriki (chain-and-staff)   154
chobatsu (right to punish)   133
Christianity
   influence on *koryu* 52
Chujo-ryu 110, 166
Collins, Kini   73 - 74, 160 - 161
combat
   philosophy and ethics of 17, 191 - 193

training for   15, 39, 97, 148, 150 - 151, 156, 182 - 183, 186
combat effectiveness   15, 18, 83
   development of   18, 166
   nature of   18, 53
   physical aspects   20, 25 - 26, 87, 90, 166
   spiritual aspects   18, 21 - 26
combat systems
   archery   154
   close-quarter   154 - 155, 168
   gunnery   154
      tanegashima   39
   koryu   149, 156, 180, 185
   See also combat, training for
combative principles   15, 53 - 54, 120
   engagement   187 - 189, 191
   harmony 21 - 25
   hasuji (trajectory and/or targeting)   110
   hyoshi/choshi (timing/rhythm) 110, 188
   intent   53, 185 - 187
   intuition 13, 22
   ki   20 - 23
   kurai (mental and physical stance)   110
   maai (distancing)   46, 110, 119, 165, 187 - 188
   mental aspects   24
   perception   22
   tai sabaki (body movement)   47
   will   21, 23, 26, 187
   yielding   26
   zanshin (a state of intense awareness and concentration)   119
commercial guilds in Japan   131 - 132, 134 - 135, 137
   commerical rights (*kenri*) 133
Confucian *Analects*
   See *Analects, Confucian (Rongo)*

Confucianism   14, 18, 30, 56
Confucius (ca. 551–479 BC)   24, 30
court, Japanese   130 - 131
cowboy   172
creation of *koryu* 146, 149, 167, 170 - 171
cultural context of *koryu*   13 - 14, 17, 93, 147, 171 - 172
curricula of *koryu*   95, 98, 158

D

daimyo (warlord)   40, 109, 112
Daito-ryu   115
Dark Ocean Society   147
degeneration of *koryu*   150 - 152, 163, 173
demonstrations of *koryu*   49, 52 - 53, 91, 96, 98 - 99, 151 - 152, 154
    Asakusa Riverside Sports Center   80, 101
    Itsukushima Shrine   99
    Okayama Kobudo Festival   99
    Shimogawa Jinja   160 - 161
    Yasukuni Shrine   99
development of *koryu*   149, 166
differences and similarities among *koryu*   155
diploma (*menkyo*)   133, 138
distancing (*maai*) 110, 165, 187 - 188
do-giri (cut to the torso)   72
domain (*han*)   38, 40, 136
    See also Aizu *han, otome ryu* (official system), Satsuma *han*, Sekiyado *han*, Tsugaru *han*
dozoku (a family and its retainers)   56 - 57
    See also social structure of *koryu*
Draeger, Donn F. (1922–1982)   36, 51 - 52, 87, 179 - 180, 185 - 187, 193
dueling systems   122, 149
duels 149, 156, 158
    etiquette   122

E

Edamatsu Kimitada   112
Edo (present-day Tokyo)
    famous dojo in   117
    travel to and from   94
Edo period (1600–1868)   112
    bureaucratic paperwork in   94
    bushi in   150
    famous swordsmen of   116
    heiho in   155
    koryu in   40, 148
    travel conditions in   94
    weapons   95
    See also Tokugawa period
education
    in pre-WWII Japan 70 - 71, 76 - 77
ego   21, 24 - 25, 152, 181
enemy   23 - 24
entrance oath in *koryu*   96
ethics in *koryu*   15, 190, 192
etiquette (*reigi, reiho*)   80, 98, 121
    dueling   122
    familial   130
extinction of *koryu*   13, 158

F

family structure in Japan   130 - 131
    commerical guilds and   133 - 135, 137
    See also *iemoto*
February 26th Incident (*Niniroku Jiken*)   63
flower arranging (*ikebana*)   51, 55 - 56, 132, 135
formlessness   23
freestyle practice of *koryu*   114, 123, 149, 165
Friday, Karl F.   15 - 16
fukuro shinai (leather-covered bamboo sword) 98
furniture, antique   41 - 42, 47
future of *koryu*   12, 60, 124, 193

Index   197

fuzoku bugei (attached arts)
See Shinto Muso-ryu, *fuzoku bugei*

G

gaikokujin (foreigners)   36
gekken (early form of bouting with bamboo swords)   149
Gembukan Dojo 117
geography and *koryu*   37, 94, 152
glaive
See *naginata*
Go Rin no Sho   170
goals of *koryu*   15, 23, 53, 57, 153 - 155, 165, 167, 173, 187, 190 - 191
grappling
systems   151
Araki-ryu 164
modern   165
techniques   152
See also *jujutsu*
gungaku (strategy and tactics)   154

H

haikai (verse)   132
hamon (formal expulsion)   133
han (domain)   38, 40, 136
harmony   21 - 25
hasuji (trajectory and/or targeting)   110
headmaster   44 - 45, 49 - 50, 74, 97, 114, 116 - 117, 122
See also *soke*
Heian period (794–1185)
bushi in   156
heiho (strategy)   154, 180
See also Shinkage-ryu
Henmi Chifuji   116
Henmi family   115, 122
Henmi Tashiro Yoshitoshi   115, 122
Higo Koryu   99, 147
Higuchi Sadakore   146
historical context of *koryu*   17, 38, 93, 147, 166

Hokushin Itto-ryu   46, 109, 114
curriculum   123
Gembukan Dojo   117
history   116 - 117
Mito Tobukan Dojo   117
Hokushin Muso-ryu   116
hono embu (formal demonstration at a shrine)   80
horagai (conch shell, used as a signaling device)   145
Hozoin-ryu   46, 147
hyoshi/choshi (timing/rhythm) 110

I

iaido
All-Japan Iaido Federation   152
development of   151
Muso Shinden-ryu   121
iaijutsu
Kashima Shinto-ryu   46, 159
Katori Shinto-ryu   46, 159
Kogen Itto-ryu   121
Shin Tamiya-ryu   117
I-ching (Book of Changes)   23, 29
ichinichi soden (temporary permission)   133 - 134
ie (extended family)   56
See also social structure of *koryu*
iemoto (family lineages) 132, 137
iemoto system (*iemoto seido*)   133 - 136
ikebana (flower arranging)   51, 55 - 56, 132, 135
Ikegami Jozaemon Yasumichi 112
Ikkaku-ryu   40, 46
Imperial Palace   63, 67
individual identity of *koryu*   49 - 50, 55, 167
innovation in *koryu*   147, 154, 166 - 167, 172
instruction 18, 25
of principles   24
technical 24
verbal   19, 22

instructors of *koryu*   51, 157, 163,
    166, 169, 171, 181
    See also *shihan, shihan-dai*
International Hoplology Society   185
Internet websites 129
Ishida Kazuto   118
ishin denshin (mind-to-mind
    transmission)   24
Iso Mataemon Masatari   117
Issai Chozan (1659–1727)   15, 18,
    25 - 27
    Inaka Soji (The Country Chuang
        Tzu)   18
    Neko no Myojutsu   18
Isshin-ryu 40
itinerant training (*musha shugyo*)   110
Ito Ittosai Kagehisa (Itto-ryu founder)
    109 - 110
Ito Masamori   112
Itto Shoden Muto-ryu 109
    curriculum   124
    history   117
Itto-ryu   13, 38, 109, 114, 124, 164
    history   109 - 110
    itto sunawachi banto 110, 118
    muso ken   110
    zetsumyo ken   110
    See also Hokushin Itto-ryu, Itto
        Shoden Muto-ryu, Kogen
        Itto-ryu, Mizoguchi-ha
        Itto-ryu, Nakanishi-ha
        Itto-ryu, Ono-ha Itto-ryu

J

Japan
    geographic characteristics of   94
Japanese family structure
    See family structure in Japan
Japanese language
    dialects   94
Japanese poetics (*waka*) 130
Japanese warriors
    See *bushi*
Jigen-ryu   40, 165

Jikishinkage-ryu   117, 124, 149
Jikishinkage-ryu (*naginata*)   71
    tsuki   72
jitoku (self-acquisition) 24
jodan (high position)   119
jodo 46, 58
    See also Shinto Muso-ryu
jojutsu (stick techniques)   121
    See also Shinto Muso-ryu
joka machi (castle town) 115
jousting   36
judo 36, 48, 152, 165, 168, 179 - 180,
    182
    Kodokan   136, 147
jujutsu   46, 48, 53, 180
    degeneration of   151
    Kata   87
    Kiraku-ryu   146
    Meiji-era 168
    Takenouchi-ryu   46, 95, 157
    Tenjin Shinyo-ryu   117
    See also Araki-ryu, Yagyu
        Shingan-ryu
junior instructors (*natori*)   132, 137
jutte (truncheon) 40, 46, 95
juttejutsu (truncheon techniques)
    Ikkaku-ryu   40, 46
    Takenouchi-ryu   95

K

kagitsuki naginata (glaive with cross-bar)
    159, 162
kago (palanquin) 115
kaiken (small dagger)   77 - 78
kaisha kempo (armored swordsmanship)
    118
Kamakura period (1185–1333)
    bushi in   156
kami (deity)   159
Kanemaki Jissai   110
Kanemaki-ryu   40
Kano Jigoro   168
Kansei period (1789–1801)   112
karatedo   36, 87

Kashima Shinden Jikishinkage-ryu
See Jikishinkage-ryu
Kashima Shinto-ryu   157
    iaijutsu 46
Kashima-Shinryu 137 - 138
kata (prearranged movement pattern)
    13, 40, 45, 81 - 82, 97, 133, 149,
    154, 187, 189
    as combat training method   146,
        187 - 188
    in demonstrations 97
    reconstruction of   158, 160 -
        161, 165 - 166
Kato Isao   192
Katori Shinto-ryu   37, 51 - 52, 95,
    148, 157
    iaijutsu   46, 158 - 159
    naginatajutsu 48
Katori Shrine   95
Keeley, Liam   12, 62, 74, 185
keiko shokon (reflecting deeply on the
    past, illuminate the present)   ii,
    15
kendo   36, 70, 72, 109, 112, 117,
    121, 151, 164
    All-Japan Kendo Federation   152
    history   13, 114, 123 - 124, 150
    ji geiko (freestyle bouting)   123
    Nihon Kendo Kata   44, 109,
        114
kendoka   44
kenjutsu (swordsmanship)   36
    Araki-ryu   164
    Chujo-ryu   110, 166
    Hokushin Muso-ryu   116
    Jigen-ryu 40, 165
    Jikishinkage-ryu   117, 124, 149
    Kurama-ryu   148
    Kyoshin Meichi-ryu117
    Maniwa Nen-ryu   146, 167
    Nen-ryu   114
    Shingyoto-ryu 117
    Shinto Munen-ryu 117
    Shinto-ryu   166
    Takayanagi Toda-ryu   114

Tatsumi-ryu   114
Ten-ryu 149
kenri (commerical rights)   133
kensho (seeing reality) 25
ki (vital energy)   21, 23
kiai (focused shout)   64, 120
kimono   81
Kinyobikai   81
Kiraku-ryu 146
kiri kaeshi 46
Kishibe Fukuo   76
Kobayashi Seiko   63 - 68, 70 - 72, 76,
    78, 82
kodachi (short sword)   118 - 119, 147,
    160, 187
Kodokan judo   136, 147
Kogen Itto-ryu   109, 148, 160
    curriculum   121 - 123
    history   114 - 116
    iaijutsu   121
    kuji (nine characters)   121
    reiho (formal etiquette)   121
    tachiainin (observer)   121
    Yobukan Dojo   115 - 116, 122
kogusoku (grappling, usually in armor)
    146
    See also Araki-ryu
koryu (classical systems)   136
    definition of   145
    See also *bugei, koryu bujutsu*
koryu bujutsu (classical martial
    traditions)   36
    See also *bugei, koryu*
kosa (position of swords crossed)   119
koto (plucked zithter)   66
ko-waza (small, intricate techniques)
    83
Kozawa family   117
kuden (oral transmissions)   130, 158,
    181
kuji (nine characters)   121
Kumagaya Araki-ryu
    See Araki-ryu, Kumagaya Araki-ryu
Kung Fu (TV series)   25
Kunii family   137 - 138
Kunii Zen'ya (1894–1966)   138

KEIKO SHOKON

kurai (mental and physical stance or preparedness)   110
Kurama-ryu   148
Kurosawa Akira   93
kusarigama (chain-and-sickle)   40, 157, 159, 163 - 164, 185
kusarigamajutsu
    Isshin-ryu   40
kyoge betsuden (transmission outside the teachings)   24
kyoju (instructors)   133
Kyoshin Meichi-ryu   117
kyuba no michi (the way of the horse and bow)   156

L

Lao-tzu   29
learning, stages of   65
Lejeune, Major General John A.   183
license
    See *menkyo* (license)
Lineberger, Pat   191
Lowry, Dave   13, 34

M

maai (distancing)   110, 165, 187 - 188
    toma 119
makimono (scrolls)   72
Maniwa Nen-ryu
    tsubame gaeshi (swallow counter)   167
    yadomejutsu (arrow blocking)   146
Marine
    See United States Marine Corps
Marishiten (Buddhist deity)   116
martial art lineages   135
martial culture, Japanese   17
Meiji period (1868–1912)
    bushi in   149
    heiho in   155
    kendo in   123, 150
    renaissance of bugei in   147, 150
    shiai in   160

Meiji Revolution   150
Mencius (Mengzi 371?–289?BC)   21, 24
menkyo (license)   133, 138, 166
    See also certification in *koryu*
menkyo kaiden (license of complete transmission)   58, 154
Mikami Araki-ryu
    See Araki-ryu, Mikami Araki-ryu
mikkyo (esoteric Buddhism)   95
military applications of *koryu*
    See modern applications of *koryu*, military
military science   18
    Western methods   155
Minamoto no Tsunemoto   115
mind-to-mind transmission (*ishin denshin*)   24
Ministry of Education, Japanese   71
Mito Tobukan Dojo   117
Miyamoto Musashi   170
Mizoguchi Shingoemon Masakatsu   112
Mizoguchi-ha Itto-ryu   109, 114
    Aizu line   113, 115
    curriculum   119 - 120
    history   112 - 113
    sayu tenka demi no hitachi   119
modern applications of *koryu*   168
    military   15, 193
modern technology
    See technology, modern
mokuroku (catalog of techniques)   72 - 73, 121, 138
monouchi (working area of the blade)   119
mubutsu (no-thingness)   22 - 23, 29 - 30
mudansha (ungraded)   182
Murakami Hideo   160
Murakami Yasumasa   118
Muromachi period (1333–1568)
    bushi in   97
    ryuha in   95
musha shugyo (itinerant training)   110
musket   145 - 146, 157
    tanegashima   39

Muso Shinden-ryu   121
Muto Masao (1925–2001)   73, 79 -
    81, 90 - 91
    See also Yagyu Shingan-ryu
Muto Mitsu   76

N

nagamaki (heavy glaive-like weapon)
    53, 156, 160, 162, 187
nagaya (long building)   115
naginata (glaive)   53, 64 - 67, 70 - 73,
    116, 147, 150, 156 - 157, 159 -
    162, 186 - 188
    in WWII physical education
        curriculum   70 - 72
    See also *kagitsuki naginata*
naginatajutsu
    Higo Koryu   99, 147
    Jikishinkage-ryu   71 - 72
    Katori Shinto-ryu   48
    Kogen Itto-ryu   121
    Tendo-ryu   48, 71 - 72
    See also Toda-ha Buko-ryu
Nakanishi Chubei Tanetada   116
Nakanishi Chuta Tanesada   114
Nakanishi Chuzo Tanetake   114, 123
Nakanishi-ha Itto-ryu   109, 117
    curriculum   120 - 121
    history   114
natori (junior instructors)   132
Neko no Myojutsu (The Cat's Eerie Skill)
    15, 18 - 25, 27
Nen-ryu   114
Neo-Confucianism   18, 29
neo-koryu ("new" classical systems)   170
    - 171
Nihon Kobudo Kyokai (Japanese
    Classical Martial Arts Association)
    49, 96
    Itsukushima Shrine   99
Nihon Kobudo Shinkokai (Society for
    the Promotion of the Japanese
    Classical Martial Arts)   49 - 50,
    63, 73 - 74, 78 - 80, 96

Asakusa Riverside Sports Center
    demonstration   80, 101
Shimogawa Jinja demonstration
    160
Yasukuni Shrine demonstration
    99
Niniroku Jiken (February 26th Incident)
    63
Nippon Budokan   90, 100, 167
    videotapes   100, 167
Nishioka Tsuneo   ii, 15, 58
Nishiyama Matsunosuke   131 - 135
Nitta Suzuyo   12, 63, 97, 160 - 164
    See also Toda-ha Buko-ryu
nodachi (massive long sword)   156
Noh theater   132
nyunanshin (pliability)   153

O

observation and subjectivity   93
observation of human movement
    emic perspective   92
    etic perspective   92 - 93
observing *koryu*   91 - 92, 96, 101
Oda Nobunaga (1534–1582)   145
odachi (long sword)   118 - 119, 121,
    187
Ogiyama Shoji   65 - 67
omote (surface level)   119
onigote (thick deerhide gauntlets)   118
    - 119, 121, 123 - 124
Ono Jiroemon Tadaaki   110
Ono Jiroemon Tadakata   112, 114
Ono Jiroemon Tadakazu   111, 114
Ono Jiroemon Tadatsune   112
Ono Jiroemon Tadayoshi   112
Ono Tadahisa   112
Ono-ha Itto-ryu   46, 95, 109, 112,
    114, 117, 119 - 121
    curriculum   118 - 119
    history   110 - 112
    kiriotoshi   119
    Tsugaru line   111

oral transmissions (*kuden*)   130, 158,
    181
Osano Jun 136 - 137
Otake Risuke   51 - 52, 157 - 158
    See also Katori Shinto-ryu
otome ryu (official system)   95, 109,
    136, 148
Otsubo Motoharu (Shiho)   79 - 80
Owari Kan-ryu 96
o-waza (powerful techniques) 83
oyoroi (full armor)   155

P

pacifism   25
pattern practice
    See *kata*
pedagogical approaches to *koryu*   45,
    179
perception
    See combative principles
personality traits and *koryu* 12, 38,
    51 - 55, 57, 81, 153, 173
philosophy of *koryu*   17 - 18, 25, 29
physical education curriculum
    in wartime Japan   70 - 72
political aspects of *koryu*   38 - 39,
    157
practitioners of *koryu*   39, 42
    in the sixteenth century 135
prearranged movement patterns
    See *kata*
preservation of *koryu*   97
principles of combat
    See combative principles
protective equipment (*bogu*) 114, 123,
    149
psychological aspects of *koryu* 153, 173

R

raku (ceramic pottery)   130
Rashomon (movie)   93
reconstruction of *koryu* 46, 73, 147,
    158 - 159, 161 - 165, 172
reigi (formal etiquette)   80

reiho (formal etiquette) 121
religion, Japanese   28
    See also Buddhism, Confucianism,
        Neo-Confucianism, Shinto,
        Taoism
Relnick, Phil   36
research in *koryu* 74
    documents   96
Rob Roy (movie) 149
ronin (unemployed former warriors)
    132
rules of engagement   189
ryuso (founder) 47

S

Sakai Shiota   160
Sakura Araki-ryu
    See Araki-ryu, Sakura Araki-ryu
Sakurai Gosuke Nagamasa   115
samurai   17, 23, 36, 134, 150, 156
    See also *bushi* (warriors)
sanbo (small wooden offering tray or
    stand)   40
Sanshin Araki-ryu
    See Araki-ryu, Mikami Araki-ryu
Sasamori Junzo 112
Sasamori Takemi 112
sasoi (inviting postures or stratagems)
    44
Satsuma *han*   165
saya (scabbard)   44
seeing reality (*kensho*)   25
seiteigata (standard forms)
    kendo   44
    naginata 71
Seiwa Emperor   115
seiza (kneeling)   95
Seki Humitake   137 - 138
sekisho (barrier gates)   94
Sekiyado *han*   18
self-acquisition (*jitoku*)   24
self-conscious thought   22
self-defense using *koryu*   82
self-development
    in *koryu*   18, 80

self-development
    in modern *budo*   80
selflessness 22 - 24
Sengoku period (1467–1568)
    bushi in   156
    military tactics   157
    ryuha in   38 - 39, 109, 148, 155
sensei
    See instructors of koryu
shamisen (three-stringed plucked lute)
    66
shiai (match)   81 - 82
    Edo period   40
    Meiji period   160
    See also freestyle practice of *koryu,*
        gekken
shidachi (doing sword) 35, 44, 119 -
    120
shihan (master teacher) 74
shihan shitsu (room for teachers)   116
shihan shitsu (room for the teachers)
    116
shihan-dai (designated representative
    instructor)   65, 74
shimai (an informal style of Noh drama)
    66 - 67
Shimizu Takaji (1896–1978)   50
Shimosa Province (present-day Chiba
    Prefecture   18
Shin Tamiya-ryu 117
shinai (bamboo swords) 114
shinai geiko (training with bamboo
    swords)   123
shinbu (divine warriorship)   29
Shindo Muso-ryu
    See Shinto Muso-ryu
Shingyoto-ryu   117
Shinkage-ryu   38, 44 - 45, 84, 95,
    109, 114, 148, 180 - 181, 183,
    185, 191 - 192
    enpi 188
    gasshi uchi   125, 188
    hassei-ho jodan 188
    kata 187
    ranken   44
    tengusho 44

Shinrasaburo Minamoto no Yoshimitsu
    115
Shinto   18, 95 - 96
Shinto Munen-ryu   117
Shinto Muso-ryu   37, 46, 50, 58
    fuzoku bugei (attached arts)   40
        Ikkaku-ryu *jutte*   40, 46
        Isshin-ryu *kusarigama*   40
        Uchida-ryu *tanjo*   40, 147
Shinto-ryu 166
Shirai Toru   114
shogi (chess)   132
Showa Emperor   63, 76
shugendo   95
Simon, Pierre and Claire   74
Skoss, Diane   11, 55, 193
Skoss, Meik   13, 55, 73 - 76, 82,
    108, 162 - 164, 185
social structure of *koryu*   15, 56 -
    58, 92, 148, 153
social structures in Japan   130, 132
    - 134
soden (initiation rituals and documents)
    133
sogo bujutsu (comprehensive martial
    arts)   157
sojutsu
    Hozoin-ryu   46, 147
    maki 186
    Owari Kan-ryu   96
soke (headmaster) 14, 63, 66, 71, 76,
    90, 164
    as family lineages   131, 134, 138
    authority of   133 - 134
    definition of   129 - 130, 134, 137
        - 138
    formal legal rights   134, 136
    responsibilities of   130, 137
soke system
    decline of   136 - 137
Sorensen, Kent   74
spear
    See *yari*
spiritual aspects of *koryu*   17, 38
Stawowy, Margaret   12, 15
strategic principles   38

Keiko Shokon

student-teacher relationship   37, 49 - 50, 130, 153, 163, 182 - 184
succession
    in family lineages   131
suhada kempo (unarmored swordsmanship)   118
suieijutsu (training in swimming for warriors in armor)   155
sumo   165
Suneya Ryosuke   160
sutekkijutsu (stick techniques)
    Uchida-ryu   147
sword
    See *tachi*
swordsmanship
    See *kaisha kempo, kenjutsu, suhada kempo*

T

tachi (sword)   64, 148, 150, 156 - 157, 159 - 160, 187 - 188
tachiainin (observer)   121
tactics in *koryu*   26
tai sabaki (body movement)   47
taijutsu (empty-handed techniques) 65
taikai
    See demonstrations of *koryu*
Taisho period (1912–1926)   112
Takayanagi-ha Toda-ryu   114
Takano Sazaburo Toyomasa   114
Takayanagi Matashiro Toshitatsu   114
Takeda family   115
Takeda Katsuyori (1546–1582) 145
Takenouchi Tojuro   94
Takenouchi-ryu   46, 95, 157
Tanba Jurozaemon Tadaaki
    See Issai Chozan
tanden (physical and spiritual center of gravity, located about 3 cm. below the navel)   20
tanegashima (matchlock musket)   39
tanjo (short stick)   40, 167
tanjojutsu
    Uchida-ryu   40, 147
tantra   130

Tao te ching   29
Taoism   18, 95
tasuki (cords used to tie back kimono sleeves)   80
Tatsumi-ryu   48, 96 - 97, 114, 157
tea ceremony (*chanoyu*) 51, 55 - 56, 132, 135
technical aspects of *koryu*   20, 95, 97, 179
technical contamination in *koryu*   43 - 45, 47 - 49, 152 - 153
technical exchange in *koryu*   40, 46
technique
    mastery of   20, 54
    neuro-muscular integration of 54
    See also *waza*
technology, modern   189 - 190, 192
Tendo-ryu   48, 71
    do-giri   72
Tenjin Shinyo-ryu   117
Ten-ryu   149
Tenshin Itto-ryu 114
tenshin sho (bequeathed by divine influence)   159
Tenshin Shoden Katori Shinto-ryu
    See Katori Shinto-ryu
Terada Gouemon   114
Toda Seigen   110
Toda-ha Buko-ryu   63 - 68, 71, 78, 97, 121, 167, 170 - 171
    betsu mokuroku (extra compendium) 162 - 164
    bojutsu (staff techniques) 161
    curriculum   159 - 160
    foreigners in   74 - 75
    future of 74, 82
    history   72, 74
    hon mokuroku (original compendium) 162, 164
    mokuroku (scrolls) 160 - 161
    teaching licenses   74, 76
Toda-ryu   147
tojutsu (swordsmanship)   110
Tokugawa
    Mito family   117
Tokugawa Hidetada (1579–1632)   111

Tokugawa Iemitsu (1604–1651)   111
Tokugawa Ieyasu (1543–1616) 38, 111
Tokugawa period (1603–1868)
    bugeisha in   40
    bureaucratic paperwork in   39
    bushi in   38
    commercial guilds in   132, 137
    cultural arts in 131, 133
    Pax Tokugawa 123, 131, 135, 146
    ryuha in   40, 123
    soke in   131 - 132, 134, 136, 138
    See also Edo period
Tokugawa shogunate   111, 146
    official kenjutsu schools of   95,
        109, 111
Tokyo
    bombing of during WWII   67,
        69
    koryu in   37
    wartime conditions   67, 69 -
        70
toma (long distance)   119
Tomoe Gozen   66
tori (taker the one who executes
    technique)   87, 90
torite (unarmed restraining techniques)
    146
training in *koryu* 26
    multiple 36 - 37, 39, 41 - 43, 45 -
        47, 49 - 52, 54 - 55, 58 - 60,
        152 - 153
    nature of 153, 180 - 181, 190, 193
training weapons   35, 87, 165
    bokuto (wooden sword) 98, 124,
        149
    fukuro shinai (leather-covered
        bamboo sword)   98
transmission of *koryu* 13 - 15, 42, 49
    - 50, 52, 74, 96 - 98, 124, 158 -
    159, 172
transmission outside the teachings
    (*kyoge betsuden*)   24
tsuba (sword guard)   161
Tsugaru Echigo-no-kami Nobumasa
    111

Tsugaru *han* (present-day Aomori
    Prefecture)   111
Tsugaru Tosa-no-kami Nobutoshi   112
tsukai sute (use-and-throw-away)   156
tsuki (thrust)   72
Tureck, Rosalyn   35 - 36, 58

U

Uchida Ryohei   147, 167
uchidachi (striking sword)   35, 44,
    119 - 121, 123 - 124
    See also *ukedachi*
Uchida-ryu   40, 147
uchigatana (light sword) 156
Ueshiba Morihei 168
uke (receiver the one on whom
    techniques are executed)   87,
    90, 157, 163
ukedachi (receiving sword)   160, 163
    See also *uchidachi*
United States Army   145
    Rangers   148
United States Coast Guard   145
United States Marine Corps   145, 180,
    186, 191 - 193
    Boot Camp   182 - 183
    Martial Art   15, 186
    Raiders   183
    rifle squad   188
ura (inner level)   119

V

verse (*haikai*)   132
victory   23, 27
violence and non-violence   17, 25 -
    26

W

waka (Japanese poetics) 130
Walker, Colonel Anthony   186
warlord (*daimyo*) 40, 109

Warring States period
    See Sengoku period
warriors, Japanese
    See *bushi*
The Way (Tao, also Do or Michi)   20,
    22 - 23
waza (technique)   118, 120
    as commerical property   133
weapons   53, 188
Westerners in *koryu*   13 - 14, 36 -
    37, 41, 43, 50 - 52, 59 - 60, 161
will   21, 23
World War II
    American occupation of Japan
                77 - 78
wrestling   165, 179

Y

yadomejutsu (arrow blocking)   146
yagoe (arrow voice)   64
Yagyu Shingan-ryu   80, 87, 95, 157
    Goto-ha   90
    kaeshi (turn over)   91
    kaiten dosa (rotation movement)
            91
    kata 87 - 90
    mukuri (turn over)   87 - 91
    terminology   94
    See also Muto, Masao (1925-2001)
yamabushi (mountain ascetics)   95
Yamaga Hachirozaemon Takami   112
Yamamoto Kunio   72
Yamaoka Tesshu (1836–1888)   114, 117,
    124
Yamaoka Tetsutaro Takayuki
    See Yamaoka Tesshu
yari (spear)   46, 53, 116, 147, 150, 156
    - 157, 159, 187
Yazawa Isao   164
Yobukan Dojo   115 - 116
yudansha (graded)   182

Z

Zama Shoko   73, 162 - 163
zanshin (vigilance upon completion of
    technique)   119
Zen   18, 24, 31, 117
zori (straw sandals)   69

Index

Koryu.com:
The Internet Resource
of the Classical Martial Arts

A unique compendium of photographs, essays, excerpts, book reviews, and more. Visit soon and take advantage of the wealth of free information we have collected, and keep up-to-date on the latest Koryu Books publications. If you'd like to read more quality books like this one, check out our special online bookstore, where you can read detailed reviews of our carefully selected recommendations, then order any title for immediate shipment. Your satisfaction with your purchase is 100% guaranteed or your money will be cheerfully refunded.

http://koryu.com/